DESERT SHADOWS

A true story of the Charles Manson Family in Death Valley

by
Bob Murphy

When the Death Valley community realized the extent of the Manson family's activities, the fear engendered was more penetrating than the deepest chill of the desert night.

Library of Congress Catalog Card Number: 93-93688

ISBN 0-930704-29-0

Cover photo by Bob Logsdon
Published by Robert Murphy

Distributed by:
    Sagebrush Press
    Post Office Box 87
    Morongo Valley, CA 92256

Foreword

Superintendent Bob Murphy in Death Valley, 1969. Robert Murphy photo.

When Robert Murphy, former superintendent of Death Valley National Monument, asked me to write a foreword to his book about the Charles Manson family and its activities in Inyo County, California, I was both pleased and honored. Bob Murphy's knowledge and understanding of the Death Valley area is equalled by few. This first-hand knowledge has enabled him to write a new and unique account of the family's life in the desert and their subsequent arrest there.

Inyo County itself is larger than the state of Vermont in area. It contains the majority of Death Valley National Monument and is a land of stark contrasts. From the peak of Mount Whitney to the desert floor at Bad Water these contrasts can be truly overwhelming. It is an apt setting for the drama of good and evil illustrated by the activities of the Manson family. It seems the desert draws prophets, saints, and sinners more than any other locality; its blue skies reflect off mountains that appear brown and dry, yet high in their reaches are lush green canyons and waters that in floodtide are swift and retributory.

When "Charlie" and his family came into Death Valley and tried to make the land their own, they had no way of knowing the tradition of pride, duty, and dedication they would encounter in the law enforcement officers there. Unlike the other books written on the Manson case, this one tells mainly the story of several highly intuitive and daring California Highway Patrol officers. Inyo County deputy sheriffs, and park rangers. If it were not for the dedication of these men, far more evil would probably have occurred in California. Having worked closely with these officers as District Attorney of Inyo County, I am pleased that finally, in this book, their work has gained the recognition it deserves.

What impresses me most about Bob's book is its thoroughness. Here on these pages you will find a wealth of detail that is a valuable contribution to the history of a fascinating and important area. The spirit in which it is written and the nature of the man who wrote it is best summed up in the last paragraph of the book. Thanks to men like Bob Murphy, "today's occasional visitor may shut off the engine of his four-wheel-drive and hear nothing, not even the sound of the wind."

Frank H. Fowles
Attorney at Law
Bishop, California

Acknowledgments

Many of the events in Death Valley that contributed to the apprehension and arrest of the Manson Family in 1969 were overshadowed
by the infamous Tate and LaBianca homicides. The lingering trials and
extensive media coverage of these murders focused world-wide attention on Los Angeles for a long time, but there were also invaluable
though little-known investigations of the Manson Family in Death Valley
that contributed greatly in the final testimonies and convictions of seven
members of the Manson Family.

Members of the California Highway Patrol (CHP), National Park
Service, Death Valley 49er's, Inc., Inyo County District Attorney's Office,
and other Inyo County officials have contributed immeasurably to this
historical account of the Family's activities in Death Valley. All of the
investigative reports, taped narratives, written reports, and letters have
made this book possible.

I would especially like to thank Ray Hailey, retired Sergeant from
the California Highway Patrol, for his enduring encouragement and
endless flow of information; Jim Pursell, California Highway Patrol
officer, for the thoroughness of his reports and the unparalleled exact-
ness of his recall, and Dave Steuber, former Auto-Theft Investigator of
California, for his lengthy tape dictated from his original field notes.
I greatly appreciate all the California Highway Patrol officers whose
input added to the depth of this story.

I thank Frank Fowles, former Inyo County District Attorney, for his
tapes and informative introduction to the book. This introduction
modestly reveals a minimum of the time and detailed effort contributed
by his office and assistants.

Thanks also go to the National Park Service; to former Chief Park
Ranger, Homer Leach, who dictated narrative reports from his original
diary of 1969, which accurately recorded times, dates, geographics,
and Family activities that might otherwise have been lost, and to Park
Rangers Dick Powell and Don Carney for their narrative reports and
extensive letters, which filled in many gaps in the story.

I am indebted to the Inyo County Sheriff's Office, expressly to Dennis
Cox whose understanding of the Family's activities contributed to the
explication of the early events in Owens Valley, and to Dee Ward

who surmounted many difficulties to fill requests for information that only her husband, Don, who died of cancer in 1976, could otherwise have answered.

I cannot express adequate appreciation to members of the Death Valley 49er's: to Joe Doctor of Exeter, California, who edited the first rough draft and made invaluable suggestions for rewriting it; George Koenig who gave continual encouragement and advice, and Hugh Tolford, production manager, who supported me during the difficult process of marketing.

Special thanks go to Vincent Bugliosi, prosecutor of the Tate-LaBianca trials, for his assistance in locating tapes, and for his encouragement.

Thanks also to my wife Alice for her constant support and efforts in typing and retyping the manuscript; to Carl Racster for her graphics, and to Bonnie Hyatt-Murphy for final editing.

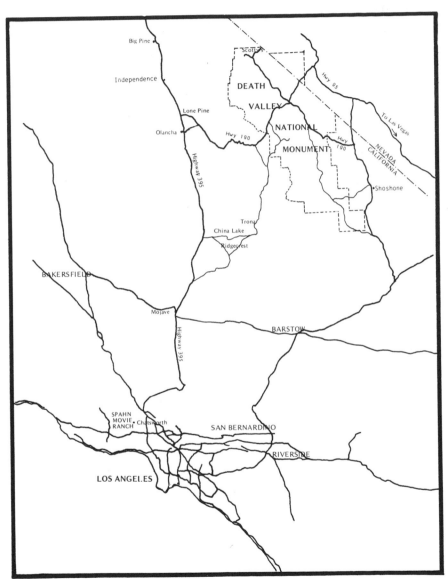

Major Route to Death Valley from Los Angeles.

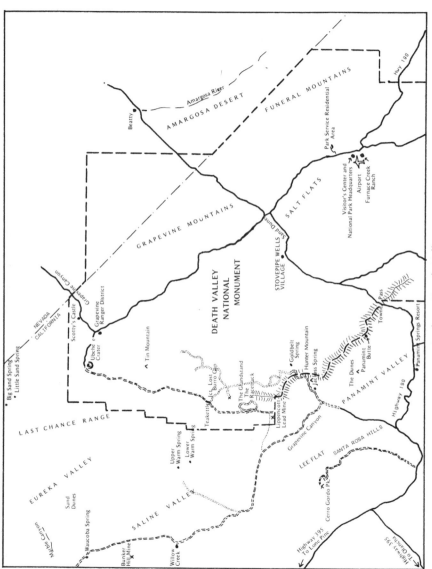

Northern Death Valley.

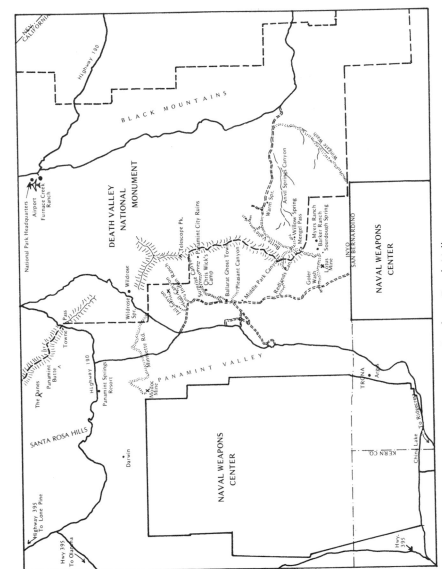

Contents

◄1►

Arson in the Desert

It was five o'clock in the morning, September 19, 1969, at the maintenance area of Death Valley National Monument at Cow Creek, three miles north of National Park Headquarters. Kirby Sims, road foreman, left his trailer home, bade his wife Margie goodbye, and drove his pickup to meet heavy equipment operator Kyle Jones at his trailer home just down the road. They drove to the equipment repair shop where Ross Boland was waiting.

Sims, who had come to Death Valley National Monument seventeen years before from Yellowstone National Park, was a true westerner. Born and reared in Wyoming, he was noted for hard work and dedication to his job.

Kyle Jonas was born in Texas and spent his early working years in New Mexico. His Texas drawl and sense of humor provided relief from the monotony and hazards of the desert.

A native Shoshone Indian who had grown up in Death Valley, Ross Boland loved the desert. As a youth he had been a caddy on the Furnace Creek Ranch golf course; he became a good golfer and a carefree, happy bachelor.

The trio headed north on Highway 190 toward Scotty's Castle and the Grapevine Ranger Station, circling the saltflats near the Beatty road and ascending above sea level. At the turnoff to Stove Pipe Wells, they left Highway 190 and continued north on the hardtop road over the alluvial fans emanating from the canyons of the Grapevine Mountains on the east. Far west across the valley, Tin Mountain was bathed in sunshine.

Shortly after 6 a.m., they passed the Grapevine Ranger Station, having come fifty-two miles. Three miles below Scotty's Castle, Sims turned left, passed Ubehebe Crater, left the narrow oiled road and proceeded on a primitive road 28 miles toward the Race Track.

This road is little traveled during the summer and when Sims reached Teakettle Junction—named for a battered metal teapot nailed to a post as a marker—he noted fresh tire tracks on the road leading south toward Lost Burro Gap and Hunter Mountain.

The trio headed southwest toward the Race Track area where they had been working with heavy road equipment. There is a rock out-

Furnace Creek Ranch, resort, National Park Service campgrounds, museum and administration building. Richard Frear photo.

crop near the edge of the playa known as the Grand Stand where, in earlier times, Indian women and children cheered for their favorite horsemen in the races for which the Race Track acquired its name. The Race Track is also noted for a phenomenon once recorded in Ripley's *Believe it or Not*: When infrequent rains accompanied by high winds cause rocks to fall from the cliffs on the south side of the playa they skid across the flat and slippery surface of the playa; then tracks are left as the winds move the rocks for a brief period of time.

Kirby Sims and his work crew had been putting up barriers on a cutoff road that descended into desolate Saline Valley, north and west of Death Valley, and signing the road as closed. This route takes off below the Race Track, an old miners' road that is next to impossible to traverse with any vehicle. Two people perished in 1967 when their pickup stalled in the 120-degree heat. With barriers and signs, at least an awareness of the potential hazard involved in traveling would be more obvious.

As the crew traveled along the west side of the Race Track, Ross Boland thought he observed smoke in the distance toward the Lippencott Lead Mine. As they approached their road maintenance equipment, Sims exclaimed, "My God—the Michigan loader is on fire."

Sims brought the pickup to a halt and ordered his crew to get the shovels from the back of the pickup and fire extinguishers from the road grader. With dirt flying from the shovels to reduce the flames, the extinguishers proved somewhat effective. Still the huge tires continued to flame up and more dirt was applied until only smoke arose from the machine.

The Michigan Articulating Loader had been purchased by the National Park Service only a few months before for nearly $35,000. It was Sims' pride and joy, and when the men could finally catch their breath, he exhorted in anger, "Who the hell would do a thing like this?"

They checked the grader, air compressor, and five-ton dump truck parked at the scene, but none seemed to have been damaged. They checked for tire tracks in the area, trying to decide in which direction the arsonists had traveled. There appeared to be two different sets of vehicle tracks. Whether they had come up out of Saline Valley or from Tea Kettle Junction and had gone down into the Saline was uncertain. In studying footprints and the nature of the tire tracks, Sims was quite certain they had come up out of Saline Valley around the rock barricade and headed out toward Tea Kettle Junction, Lost Burro Gap, and probably Hunter Mountain.

The Michigan loader started to flame up again and more dirt was shoveled on the tires. The men noted that a fuel line had been cut and diesel fuel had been drained from the tank. A nearby fuel can contained what smelled like diesel fuel and gasoline. Whoever was responsible for burning the machine had probably mixed diesel oil and gasoline to ignite the tires and wiring.

"We had better call Carney on the radio and see if he can come up here," Sims said. "Maybe we can catch up with these bastards."

Don Carney was the district ranger for the north end of Death Valley, a bachelor living at Grapevine Ranger Station. He was a cool, collected and meticulous individual. As an investigating officer he was as intelligent as he was competent and thorough. His assistant was Ranger Clifford "Rocky" McCreight, also a bachelor who lived in a nearby apartment across the road and below the ranger station. Rocky had a western air about him and was also a very perceptive young man.

In calling Carney, Sims told him, "Somebody burned the loader, yeah, the Michigan. They set it on fire. We put it out. Can you come up right away?"

Carney noted the time, 7:20 a.m., and within ten minutes he and McCreight were headed for the Race Track. The day was clear and the early morning temperature a balmy seventy-five degrees. When the rangers arrived the loader was still smoking. They checked the area and decided to pursue the direction the suspected vehicles were traveling. Sims left Boland to stand watch over the parked equipment

Death Valley from south end of Panamint Mountains. Robert Murphy photo.

with instructions to be on the lookout for any strangers and "to get on the radio if anyone shows up."

Sims and Jonas joined the rangers following the tire tracks. They found where the suspects had stopped on the Race Track playa, apparently to change a tire. The four followed the tracks back to Tea Kettle Junction, then south to Lost Burro Gap. Here Carney called park headquarters at Furnace Creek, relating the situation and suggesting an air patrol of the area. He also radioed Ranger Dick Powell at Wildrose Ranger Station, instructing him to proceed into Panamint Valley to the junction of Highway 190 and to the Hunter Mountain road west of Death Valley, because the tracks appeared to head in that direction. Rocky McCreight recognized the odd tire tread they were following as a standard type provided for a 4x4 Toyota.

Just before arriving at Goldbelt Springs, the search party found a red shovel on one of the tire tracks. The vehicle was evidently traveling fast enough for the shovel to bounce out. Through a maze of side roads, the search party went up over Hunter Mountain and started down the west side. Suddenly the tracks turned off into a faint side road near Jackass Spring. Here they found a new green 1969 Ford sedan crashed into a pinion pine tree, and old clothing and shoes at what appeared to be the remnants of a hippie camp. Subsequent investigation disclosed that this vehicle was rented from Hertz Corporation in

Los Angeles by a Penelope Tracy, using a Mobile credit card that had been reported stolen to the Los Angeles Police Department September 7, 1969. The name Penelope Tracy turned out to be an alias used by Nancy Pitman, one of Charles Manson's family.

Sims and Jonas returned to the place where the loader had been burned. Ross Boland, who uneasily guarded the equipment, had not seen anyone since his companions had left early in the morning. Ross asked, "What would I have done if those guys had come back, run over them with the damned truck?" Jonas jokingly replied, "Hell, no, Ross, we thought you'd scalp 'em."

Sims told the others that Chief Ranger Leach was coming up to check out the loader for prints and to make some plaster casts of tire tracks. Sims remained on the site while Boland and Jonas took the truck below toward the Saline Valley cut-off road to pick up some tools and tow up the compressor.

Carney and McCreight went out toward Highway 190 and joined Powell a few miles down below. The odd tire tracks of one vehicle were easily visible on the soft soil around Jackass Spring, but out on the rocky flats where they met Powell, they became indistinct. Powell told them there were a number of tire tracks entering the south approach to Saline Valley down Grapevine Canyon, and it was assumed the suspected vehicles would have gone back down this route.

National Park Service Visitor Center and administration office building. Furnace Creek National Park Service photo.

Having seen no other vehicles in the area, active mines, or people living in the vicinity who might be witnesses, the rangers decided to recheck the entire route. They thought they might have missed some of the side roads where the suspects could have turned off. Carney and McCreight went back over the entire route to the Race Track, checking out all the side roads.

Chief Ranger Leach, in his office at the Visitors' Center at Furnace Creek, after monitoring early morning radio traffic, had sent Ranger Lou Hendricks out to check out northern Panamint Valley and to join Powell west of Hunter Mountain.

California Highway Patrolman Jim Pursell, who lived at Furnace Creek, was en route with his wife and five-year-old son to Lone Pine, a hundred or so miles west of Death Valley, to do some shopping. Pursell had a National Park Service hand radio in his car and was monitoring the radio traffic. He left his family at Panamint Springs Resort, and joined Hendricks and later Powell. They all went over the route, searching from Highway 190 back to Hunter Mountain.

Pursell checked out the green Ford sedan for vehicle identification and called the license number SOZ 976 into the California Highway Patrol office in Bishop for a stolen auto check. The right rear wheel and tire and the spare wheel and tire were missing. CHP in Bishop would send Officer Doug Manning from Lone Pine to remove the Ford and store it as an abandoned vehicle although the car had not been reported stolen at this time.

At mid-morning, Chief Ranger Leach had a visit from Boyd Taylor, U.S. Commissioner from Bishop, at the Visitors Center. Taylor was an avid desert camper and was passing through on a camping trip. He had stopped to say hello; then he heard the radio messages regarding a fire at Race Track.

He told Leach that he had camped the previous evening at one of the Warm Springs in Saline Valley and had met and talked with a bunch of hippies there. They were driving a red Toyota and a couple of dune buggies. They had indicated plans to take a back road up to the Race Track. The vehicle descriptions were broadcast to the field units.

Ranger Schneider, located at Park Headquarters, arranged for a pilot and a patrol plane out of Las Vegas and was over Hunter Mountain by 10 a.m. They circled the area several times and flew down over the loader and the Race Track, but observed no vehicles in the area. Over Saline Valley he received Leach's description of the vehicles, a red Toyota, and a dune buggy. At Lower Warm Springs were people and vehicles. Hippies and vehicles were also at Willow Creek and Waucoba Springs, but no red Toyota was observed.

Schneider then flew down Marble Canyon and over Eureka Valley.

Panamint Valley, Goler Wash, right of center. National Park Service photo.

No vehicles were observed at the large sand dunes. They then proceeded out over the Last Chance Range and into the north end of Death Valley checking out Big and Little Sand Springs, with no luck. The air route then took them over Scotty's Castle, Ubehebe Crater, the Race Track and back to Hunter Mountain.

Schneider decided to recheck the Warm Springs in Saline Valley, knowing that a red vehicle could be hidden easily in that locality, and then he flew to the north end of Panamint Valley in the vicinity of The Dunes and Panamint Buttes. Nothing suspicious caught his eye, but he was back in the air that afternoon after refueling at Furnace Creek Airport.

Later, Leach drove to the Race Track, taking pictures of the loader, dusting for prints, and making plaster casts of the suspect tire track. Rangers Carney and McCreight joined Leach at the Race Track and searched for clues. Carney picked up an empty match book with psychedelic colors and the word "Northwoods" printed on it. Later this would be found to be a restaurant in the Los Angeles area.

In the afternoon, Powell and Hendricks were sent back to check out the road in Grapevine Canyon and mining roads in the Santa Rosa Hills and Lee Flat below the Cerro Gordo mine. By the end of the day they had traveled over a series of treacherous desert roads.

Later that evening Chief Ranger Homer Leach sat by the burned loader in the fading light of evening wondering if the story of its burning would ever be fully known.

◄2►
Search,
Bewilderment
& Intrusion

On September 20, Rangers Carney and Powell were sent into Saline Valley to locate and interview anyone they could find and check the Warm Springs area for signs of hippies.

Park Service Roads Foreman Chuck Tobin was scheduled to fly the area again, using a rented plane from Las Vegas. He and the pilot took off from the Furnace Creek Airport and again covered the Hunter Mountain and Race Track area. Tobin contacted Carney and Powell down in Saline Valley when he was over the Warm Springs area, but he couldn't detect any vehicles in the vicinity. Later in the morning he reported to the rangers seeing vehicles in the north end of Saline Valley, but no red Toyota.

September 20 happened to be the opening day of deer season, so when CHP Officer Manning was sent to check out the green Ford at Jackass Spring, and the roads were in bad shape, he parked his CHP cruiser and rode in with two deer hunters, Joe Davis and Melvin Chico of Darwin, the mining community west of Panamint Valley. They were driving a 4x4 Chevrolet and helped Manning check out the green sedan. Later, a wrecking service was called to move the vehicle from the area. The hunters related to Manning that they had recently seen hippies driving the Ford sedan in the flats near Darwin in the Argus Range accompanied by a red 4x4 Toyota and a dark-colored dune buggy.

Carney and Powell were down in Saline Valley doing some back-tracking. At the junction of the main Saline Valley road and the Race Track cutoff, which had been blocked off and signed "closed", they found the Toyota tire tracks which turned north and were eventually lost in a maze of other tracks. As a result, the rangers methodically checked out every side road on their way north.

In the vicinity of the sand dunes and Warm Springs, there were tracks everywhere but no witnesses were located. On their last stop far to the north at active Bunker Hill mine, the rangers saw several buildings and trees, and for the first time in their long search, people as well. It was about 5 p.m. and some of them were preparing to eat dinner. Two of three revealed little except that there were hippies in the area recently. Suddenly, Carney recognized a familiar face belonging to a slight blond-haired fellow of about forty with a face and disposition of a mouse and just as furtive. He was a former employee at Scotty's Castle and one of the "poor sheep" that Manager Basil Wickett had sheared in the spring of 1967. If his employees wouldn't walk the line, Wickett had a unique way of sending them down the road: He subjected them to a "shearing."

The fellow recognized Carney and told the rangers to go back to the Warm Springs road and look again. He said, "Drive as far as you can up those side roads." On a side road at Upper Warm Springs they found the Toyota tracks and at the end of the road was a campfire. Two hippies, a man and a woman, sat by the fire in old clothes. The man had long, scraggly hair. Powell had his .38-caliber revolver lying on the front seat beside him.

The officers left their vehicle and as they approached, the man said, "I thought your jurisdiction ended about eight miles over that way." He said that he and his wife were there to get away from regulations and people. The rangers told him what had happened and why they were there. With that the man became cooperative and introduced himself as Danny R. Jones from the Southeast Law Center at Norwalk and said he had been a law partner of F. Lee Bailey and Melvin Belli. He reported seeing the hippies they were looking for, but not close up. From his campsite he had seen two or three vehicles, a large fire, and people moving around in the dark, like shadows in the night. He thought one vehicle was a red Toyota. In looking around the area that Jones pointed out, Carney found another "Northwoods" matchbook and Powell found one marked "Ralph's Market." Jones later wrote Carney several letters after learning the identity of the people he had camped near. He said his wife was so scared she would never go back to the desert.

Powell and Carney left Warm Springs after dark, traveling via Eureka Valley and into Grapevine Ranger Station about midnight. On September 21, Chief Ranger Leach drove through Panamint Valley and over Hunter Mountain to the Race Track to go over the route the hippies were known to have traveled. He also rechecked the burned loader site. At the Panamint Springs Resort he stopped for gas and talked to attendant Tex Brothers. He told Tex they were looking for some traveling hippies who were possibly camping in the area. Tex told Leach he had seen a red Jeep and a dune buggy traveling east past the resort early in the morning of September 19.

Powell checked out the maze of mining roads around Darwin and upon his return he stopped to talk to the employees of the state highway station above Panamint Springs, who had been working on Towne's Pass on the 19th. They had not seen the Toyota or dune buggies. Powell surmised the suspects had probably turned south on the Trona road into the vast area on the west side of Panamint Valley south of Panamint Mountains toward Ballarat and Trona.

On September 22, Schneider and Powell were sent in separate vehicles into Panamint Valley in a continuing effort to apprehend the persons who burned the loader. Schneider went over Towne's Pass and down the floor of Panamint Valley, then east below Indian Ranch and up into Surprise Canyon. There were some people around Chris Wicht Camp but none were identified as the type he was looking for. He went on up the steep and rocky road to the site of Panamint City, a mining camp dating back to the 1870s. There were a number of hippie's camped at various locations with a variety of vehicles. Some had dune buggies, while others had 4x4 Jeeps, but none had a red Toyota.

In conversations with these people, the ranger learned that some were students on vacation, one was a college professor collecting geological samples, and a few were a bit vague about their reasons for being in the area. Schneider reported that in his opinion, "None of these people exhibited a behaviour that might relate toward suspicion of arson."

Powell, traveling alone, entered Jail Canyon to ascertain if there were hippies in that area. He stopped first at a gold mine in the canyon east of the Hall Canyon turnoff and talked to Mrs. Inez Troster, previous owner of the mine, and Keith Cummerfeld, caretaker. They had seen and talked to a group of hippies, driving a red Toyota and a rail-type dune buggy, on the afternoon of September 19. On the morning of September 22, one vehicle had reportedly left the area.

Powell then drove to a spring in Hall Canyon where people frequently camped to enjoy the shade trees and fresh water. At the campsite he found a red 4x4 Toyota and six unkempt people, two men who later proved to be Robert "Scotty" Lane and Gary Tufts, and four women, Diane Bluestein, Rachel Morris and two that were identified later as part of the Manson family.

Powell indicated only that he was on routine patrol of the back country. He shared his lunch and cigarettes with them and answered their questions about surviving in the desert. The two men inquired about hot springs and Powell described those in Saline Valley and their locations. Despite their questions, the men appeared to be little interested in these springs, and this reaction led Powell to believe these people had previously been in that area.

The ranger attempted to gain information that might have related to their having traveled through the Race Track or Hunter Mountain area. He learned very little. He borrowed a book of matches marked "Ralph's Market," which he kept.

After visiting with the group for about an hour, one of the hippies signaled to someone in the bushes behind Powell. A young woman, later determined to be Nancy Pitman, emerged from the bushes carrying a long hunting knife in her right hand. She hesitated, as if expecting a reaction from Powell, and then put her knife away in a leather sheath on her belt. They all wore long hunting knives, and one of the hippies told Powell that Pitman had been set out there to "watch him."

After a while Powell surreptitiously wrote down the license number of the Toyota. It appeared that any opportunity to obtain additional information was negligible and Powell decided to leave the area as gracefully as possible, the nearly vertical walls of the canyon making radio communication with park headquarters virtually impossible.

Upon his return home to Wildrose, he radioed the Toyota license number to park headquarters, and the chief ranger radioed back that the vehicle had not been reported stolen through the National Crime Information Center. He said he would try to get Powell some support from the county sheriff's office to go back into the area the following day while checking further with the state's registration people on the license number of the red Toyota.

The following morning the sheriff called Leach to tell him that he would not have a deputy available until early on September 24. Late in the afternoon of September 23, Leach radioed Powell that the license plate on the red Toyota was registered to a four-wheel drive Dodge Power Wagon that belonged to Gail Beausoleil of the Los Angeles area. Later it was found that she was the wife of Robert Beausoleil who was being held as a suspect in the Los Angeles jail, charged with the murder of a music teacher, Gary Hinman.

On September 24 Ranger Powell met Deputy Sheriff Dennis Cox, who had had earlier contact with hippies in the Olancha area of Owens Valley. Deputy Cox was thought to have additional information that could be of help if the suspected people offered resistance in a possible arrest. Powell and Cox drove to Jail Canyon Mine. Mrs. Troster told the officers that the people they were seeking had left Hall Canyon about three hours after Powell's departure on September 22. She said she was glad they left, that "they sure didn't appear very trustworthy."

Powell and Cox checked potential camping areas in both Hall and Jail Canyons with no result. They went down Jail Canyon to Ballarat

Goler Wash country. Robert Murphy photo.

where the owners of the store indicated that a number of hippies had recently stopped to make some purchases. They suspected that many of them were camped out on the west side of the Panamint Range.

California Highway Patrol Officer Pursell was also in Panamint Valley for two days checking mining roads on the west side of the valley. He went to the Minnetta and Modoc mining areas seeking various locations where people might be camping in isolated areas. He learned that most of the hippies were likely to be in Surprise, Middle Park, and Pleasant canyons. There was also a report about hippies having been seen in the Goler Wash area in the southwest corner of Death Valley National Monument.

The route up out of Panamint Valley was considered inaccessible even with a four-wheel-drive vehicle because of flood damage in February of 1969. The only possible vehicle access was likely to be on the east side of the Panamint Range through Butte Valley within the boundary of Death Valley National Monument.

The officers were exhausted from their search over the vast desert area. They had covered every conceivable canyon and wash, probed on foot and through air surveillance every sand dune and cactus. Disheartened, they agreed to pursue a periodic search that might eventually be productive, but worried that the hippies they sought had already eluded justice and returned to the Los Angeles area.

Overlooking Butte Valley from Panamint Mountains. Robert Murphy Photo.

◄3►
A Hippie Contagion

During the spring and summer of 1967, the word was out all over America to come to San Francisco for free love and flowers. The psychedelic revolution was born, and California was flooded with a new group of people the press labeled hippies. Haight-Ashbury, one of the run-down older residential sections of San Francisco, was engulfed in the frenzy. All over the United States there were love-ins, outdoor rock concerts, and abundant flowers. Powerful forces were changing American youth. Nonconformists, essentially anti-war and anti-establishment, were condemning the trend toward what they believed would become a nuclear holocaust. Disregarding society's rules, young people lived and loved in streets and parks. Life they said, was meant to be free. The drug scene began with moderation but proliferated into hostility and violence. The leadership of this "new America" may have had some intellectual superiority, but the acid-dropping children and followers of this leadership were vulnerable.

The free lifestyle movement attracted a criminal element with a profit motive. Cultists, satanists, death freaks, and other vicious confidence types took over community "crash pads." Dope, rip-offs, racial problems and killings haunted the good intentions of the altruistic new movement. Brutality gained a terrible momentum and finally a reaction set in, and the disillusioned sought other interests with less grim and fatal outcomes. They traveled east to the desert and mountains.

As twilight descended over the Mojave Desert, the occasional flicker of headlights became a more-frequent occurrence than it had been in previous summers. Rural areas having scant population and the freedom of isolation attracted many who wished to escape the predatory metropolitan scene. Early in June of 1968, temperatures became extremely hot, 110 to 116 degrees. Who were the wanderers of the desert who sought the cool of the evening to travel to their destinations? Why were they there? Some traveled east to the Colorado River, others to Owens Valley, Panamint Valley, and Death Valley. They were largely a young generation of Americans operating under a set of rules they had made themselves.

As school ended in California, the exodus to the desert became a mass migration, a contagion, calling many college students, runaways and "nature children". They were largely long-haired, blue-jeaned, and seeking isolation and freedom from world problems.

In the Simi Hills north of Los Angeles a group of young hippies were preparing for an extended trip to Death Valley. They had been staying for awhile at the dilapidated Spahn Movie Ranch, a former early western movie set. It was currently used daily as a horse rental spot for pseudo cowboys needing riding practice. It was nearing the end of October when the group of seventeen adults and two babies headed out toward the Santa Susana Pass road. Their old bus had been reconditioned, the seats removed, and mattresses, curtains and psychedelic accouterments installed. One of the wranglers at the Spahn Ranch said, "Looks like a friggin' whorehouse."

This group, later called "the Family," camped the first night in a canyon in San Bernardio County, near Cajon Pass. The following morning the Family was off at sunup, driving north on Highway 395, east to Ridgecrest and east again to Trona, north along the east side of the Argus Mountains and into Panamint Valley. At this point the true impact of the hostile desert became real, with the barren Panamint Mountain Range rising 11,000 feet above the arid valley on the east side. The sun blazed off the land and heat waves shimmered on its surface; yet high up on the mountain at timberline, inviting canyons of pinion pine changed the barren landscape and made the group travel on.

Cathy Gillies, seventeen, was a bit overweight, with a pixie face and flaxen hair. She had joined the Family two months earlier and had mentioned that her grandmother, Mrs. Bill Myers, had a ranch located in the desert just south of the boundary of Death Valley National Monument. Her favorable description of the place prompted the group to go there.

It was late afternoon by the time they drove through Ballarat, a one-store outpost at the edge of the Panamint Valley floor. From there they went south, deeper into the valley toward Goler Wash. For the next fifteen miles the bus swayed and weaved over an unimproved road through sparse mesquite, desert holly and cactus until they finally arrived on a plateau at the base of Goler Wash and parked the bus beside the remaining foundation of a miner's cabin. Here they began their back-packing ascent through the rocky slit in the mountain to the Myers place.

So the first of many treks up Goler Wash began. Two of the girls carried their infants strapped to their backs. Others backpacked or carried bags of supplies—bedding, food, water and personal effects—up the wash. The ascent up lower Goler Wash was difficult; it necessitated climbing up over a series of treacherous dry rock falls, a slow, tedious climb to the flood-damaged remnants of an old mining road.

Myers Ranch, looking northwest. Robert Murphy photo.

Halfway up, the canyon widened out, becoming green with clusters of honey mesquite along the drainage route. They filled their canteens from a spring beside a deserted miner's cabin. Farther on, they passed the inactive Lotus mine perched on the mountain to their right. The road forked at Sourdough Spring, the left fork proceeding north over Mengel Pass and into Death Valley National Monument. The fork straight ahead led first to the Barker Ranch and then to the Myers Ranch. Realistically, both properties were mining claims and not ranches in the strictest definition of the term.

At the top of the wash they hiked up a narrow road past the apparently vacant Barker Ranch where there was a low rock dwelling secluded behind cottonwood and decaying fruit trees. A little more than a quarter of a mile beyond, the Family arrived at the Myers place, a small, unpretentious two-bedroom house with a fireplace. The location faced an open expanse of rolling, sparsely-covered desert. Surrounding the house were tamarisk and cottonwoods. In the backyard were remnants of a family orchard of apple and fig trees. The Family had hiked for nearly three hours to arrive at the Myers Ranch.

The following morning they divided into scouting parties, hiking the roads and trails through the mountains above the ranch. To the northeast they could look down on the floor of Death Valley. To the right, the landscape fell away into Amargosa Valley. Beyond was the thread-like road to Shoshone and Tecopa and the highway to Las Vegas; the most arid and rugged portion of the Great American Desert lay before them, three hundred and sixty degrees of tortured, tumultuous, serene, and undisputed wilderness.

Death Valley forms but a part of the Great Basin of the Great American Desert, an incredibly arid trough where salt flats slope down to 282 feet below sea level. North and south, Death Valley stretches 130 miles, widening and narrowing between vast alluvial fans poured forth from the mouths of mountain canyons. The Black, the Funeral, and the Grapevine ranges rear up on the east side in spectacular but sombre colors six to eight thousand feet high. On the west, the Panamints rise thousands of feet even higher, dominated by 11,000-foot Telescope Peak, summits bright with snow for half the year. The valley is actually the sink of Amargosa River. Not one of the streams that flow down the slopes into the valley ever reaches the sea. It is a land of upside down rivers, with stream beds on top and water beneath the sand and gravel.

This phenomenon fascinated the Family, especially Charlie Manson, their leader, who began speaking of a possible "hole" or opening in the desert that would lead to water, shelter, and a place to live in security removed from the turmoil and chaos of modern society— a subterranean world. Combining the prophecy foretold in Chapter 9 of the Book of Revelation with an Indian legend called "The Emer-

Telescope Peak, Death Valley. National Park Service photo.

Barker Ranch house, looking north. National Park Service photo.

gence of the Third World," and elaborating these stories with an acid trip vision, Manson evolved a prediction of his "Bottomless Pit." The entire mystique of subterranean worlds and infinite space was much more palatable surrounded by the silences of the desert. The cosmic vacuum of the desert was an ideal place to program young minds with Charlie's philosophy, what became infamously known as "Helter Skelter."

Shortly after noon on the third day, the Family gathered at the head of Goler Wash at the Barker Ranch. This ranch, though more spacious than the Myers place, was also built in the midst of dense, oasis-like vegetation. It was in a state of extreme neglect, including vineyard, fruit and shade trees. The rock house had a small living room, a bedroom, a dilapidated bathroom, and a large kitchen. It lacked a fireplace and depended on heat from a custom-made oil drum wood stove and an old kitchen range with an oven.

On the off side of the main ranch house was a bunkhouse made of railroad ties. In general, the Barker house was more weather-beaten and somehow more conducive to the plans the family had been dreaming. The place was completely deserted except for a prospector who occasionally slept there in his wanderings around the Panamint Mountains. Charlie had an uneasy feeling about the Myers place, because Cathy's grandmother was under the impression the group was all girls.

The Family moved into the Barker Ranch and a few days later a prospector, "Ballarat Bob," showed up with a friend. He could not believe it when he found nude hippies living in his building. There was nothing he could do about the invasion because of the remoteness of the area and lack of any formal agreement with the owner. He did suggest that the Family get permission to occupy the ranch from Mrs. Barker, who lived down the valley at Indian Ranch north of Ballarat. The prospector hoped that permission would be denied and that with the departure of the hippies, he and his partner could resume, uninhibited, their prospecting of the area.

On about November 1, two male Family members hiked down Goler Wash and drove to Indian Ranch. There they found Mrs. Barker in a weather-tight cabin surrounded by tamarisk trees. She lived alone most of the time and that morning was seated on her front porch, dozing with a newspaper in her lap. Charlie wasted no time in telling her about his accomplishments as a musician.

"You know, I've done some music for the Beach Boys. We need solitude to do our music—to get our thing together. Up here on the mountain at your ranch—it's a real pretty place to compose music, best I've seen," is the way Charlie explained his needs to her. Mrs. Barker nodded her consent and said she was willing to let them stay at the ranch for a little while on condition that they keep the place in order and fixed what needed fixing. To impress Mrs. Barker further, he gave her a framed gold record by the Beach Boys cut by Capitol Records. What Charlie did not reveal was the number of people who would be staying at the Barker Ranch, and for how long.

In the next days the Family gained access to other vehicles in addition to the bus, and scoured the desert country. Various members in small parties camped in every major canyon in the Panamint Mountains. Trips were made throughout the Death Valley region and members were later to be remembered in the small communities of Shoshone, Tecopa, and Trona as well as places in Owens Valley. Members frequently returned to Los Angeles to renew supplies of marijuana, hashish and acid. By avoiding contacts with the public, their presence in the desert isolation was little noticed. Their mode of living, rough appearance and frequent nudity served as a repulsive buffer with desert travelers and some of the miners in the locality. The presence of other hippie groups in the desert further diminished observation or any real identification of the Family.

Although the Family was reported living on the Barker Ranch in late 1968, members appeared to be absent for extended periods of time. In November, several were back and forth to the Los Angeles area.

Striped Butte in Butte Valley. National Park Service photo.

Others were at Topanga Canyon for Thanksgiving and back at the Barker Ranch for Christmas.

At about 3:30 a.m. on December 30, 1968, seventeen-year-old Marina Habe, daughter of writer Hans Habe, was abducted outside the West Hollywood home of her mother as she was returning home from a date. On new Year's day, her body was found off Mulholland near Bowmont Drive. Multiple stab wounds in the neck and chest caused her death. The victim had been acquainted with members of the Family.

By December 31, 1968, Charlie, accompanied by Family members, returned to the desert, driving the green and white bus from Los Angeles through Butte Valley in Death Valley National Monument, arriving at Barker Ranch late that evening. The road over Mengel Pass would test the endurance of a four-wheel-drive vehicle. The bus suffered slashed tires, dented fenders, gashed sides, and a bashed muffler. One of the members at Barker Ranch was reported to have exclaimed, "It was a wreck and sounded like a tractor." There by the ranch house it remained, a dead issue.

Winter soon arrived at Barker Ranch and to those accustomed to Los Angeles climate, it was cold as hell. Inadequate preparation for the cold made the Family members miserable, irritable and obviously neither mentally or physically capable of coping with this bleak

Charlie's bus, Barker Ranch. National Park Service photo.

phase of desert life. They started drifting back to Los Angeles, some in a Dodge Power Wagon and others in an acquired Jeep. A van was sent from Los Angeles to the mouth of Goler Wash in Panamint Valley to pick up the remaining Family members and return them to a house Charlie had rented at 20910 Gersham Street in Canoga Park. By January 10, 1969, only Brooks Poston and Juanita Wildebush remained in Goler Wash. Soon they too would be in Los Angeles and about the only thing left in the desert was the broken-down green and white bus parked in the yard by a tree on the Barker Ranch.

In January, there was excessively heavy snowfall in the high country of Death Valley and by February, there were snow avalanches off the Panamint Mountains, followed by flooding down the canyons. Lakes formed on the floor of Death Valley as the flooding peaked during the last days of the month. Furnace Creek recorded 2.52 inches of rain in February, the normal yearly average.

Climatologists reported that this was the greatest accumulation of moisture in nearly a hundred years. All roads were severely damaged, especially those in the Panamint Range. Later many observers wondered how the Family bus ever made it to the Barker Ranch, but it had been driven in before the runoff began. The flooding in February of 1969 gutted canyons and destroyed miles of mining roads, some built by hardy souls who in their place left a consortium of boulder fields.

Flood water, May 1969 near Stovepipe Well. Robert Murphy photo.

Badwater, flood water June 5, 1969. Robert Murphy photo.

Primitive roads that were passable in 1968 when the bus came to the Barker Ranch were by 1969 no longer in existence, destroyed by rushing waters.

◄4►
Inyo County Reacts

During the latter part of 1968, in the quiet desert town of Shoshone just south of Death Valley, there were incidents of pot smoking among high school students. Deputy Sheriff Don Ward, on duty in this small town, served as eyes and ears of the community. Don, about five-foot-three, was built like a square-shouldered bulldog. He was well-liked by the youth of the area. District Attorney Frank Fowles said that Don was the smallest man in law enforcement in the county, a truly .45-caliber officer built on a .22-caliber frame. When Deputy Don Ward reported from his office, "Somebody is pushing hash around here and they better knock it off," everyone in the community heard him.

Ward was suspicious of the hippies hanging around Shoshone and especially of the girls that frequently came in from Goler Wash and the Barker Ranch. Don's niece, Debbie, from Los Angeles was living with the Ward family and attending high school in Shoshone. Don's wife, Dee, worked at the drug store. Late one afternoon one of Don's daughters, at their home, called him and said that the hippie girls were in the yard and had just driven off with Debbie. Ward caught up with the Jeep they were driving at the Amargosa River crossing and retrieved his niece, issuing a stern warning to the hippie girls.

Later, some of this group from Goler Wash were back in town to entertain local youths. Ward was upset, because they had previously dispensed marijuana to some of the town's young people and had been warned about panhandling in the Crow Bar saloon and shoplifting in the general store. He stopped a group of them in the town section and issued them a warning. One of the men, named Charlie, challenged his authority and Ward lined him up against one of the town buildings, searched him, and then told him to get out of town and not come back. By late January, 1969, visits of the Goler Wash hippies to Shoshone ceased and Ward was curious about their absence.

Subsequently, Ward and a part-time deputy, Cliff Riggs, drove into Death Valley to the Warm Spring Miner's Camp. Miners there told them the road through Butte Valley had been pretty well flooded out. There was no way the sheriff's flatland patrol vehicle could make it into Goler Wash and Barker Ranch. Ward, not about to give up, called Leach at Death Valley National Monument. Leach had helped before and had a couple of four-wheel-drive vehicles that could make it up the Wash. On March 16, Ward, accompanied by Cliff Riggs, met Leach and Park Ranger John DolleMolle at Warm Springs in the early morning light.

The trip through Butte Valley, over Mangel Pass and down Goler Wash was a hair-raising experience, but the men finally arrived at the Barker Ranch in the early forenoon. They found only two individuals, a young woman, Juanita, and a man, Brooks Poston, living there. Both were noncommittal, disclaiming any knowledge of the Shoshone incident. They said others had been living at the ranch but had returned to the Los Angeles area. Ward warned them that anyone caught pushing pot in Shoshone would "find his ass in jail." There was some doubt in Ward's mind that these two young people were involved, so the officers left the ranch on more amiable terms.

During May and June of 1969, park rangers in Death Valley National Monument observed and contacted a number of hippies camping in the desert. Most moved up in the higher mountains to escape the torrid heat of the floor of Death Valley. By late summer, Deputy Ward noted frequent visits by the hippies coming for supplies. Deputy Sheriff Dennis Cox and Game Warden Vern Burandt declared, "Owens Valley is full of 'em." Because these people traveled in so many types of vehicles and nearly all of them exhibited a scruffy appearance, it was difficult to distinguish between those enjoying the desert as students and those on the drug route.

Subsequent checks by Ward with miners in the area produced reports that only occasionally were the hippies traveling in and out of Goler Wash. Because they avoided gathering in Shoshone, and their travel was sporadic, Ward's interest temporarily waned. Ward learned that miners Paul Crockett and Bob Berry had been prospecting in Goler Wash since early April and were reported to be staying at the Barker Ranch. Ward's logical assumption was that the Family had moved out permanently and had returned to the Los Angeles area.

Paul Crockett, in his mid-forties, had spent most of his adult life mining in the southwest. He was typical of his breed: independent, observant, a man who minded his own business; he was quiet and reticent in nature. His partner, Berry, in his thirties, shared a common interest in prospecting in the desert. His respect for Crockett was amplified by the opportunity to learn the skills of the trade.

When the miners arrived at the Barker Ranch, they were surprised to find a pair of hippies living there. The miners temporarily moved into the bunkhouse adjacent to the larger house and frequently visited with the rather exotic pair. They learned that the girl was a young runaway named Juanita Wildebush. Brooks Poston was a slender, rather docile eighteen-year-old who acted like a zombie most of the time.

Evening conversations invariably turned to the Family and to its apparent leader, a person named Charlie. The miners couldn't believe what they were hearing; in fact, it was mind-boggling, and they thought the stories were totally ridiculous. It was obvious to Crockett that these youths believed Charlie to be Christ in his second coming. Equally bewildering, they expressed considerable fear of the man.

Crockett came to the conclusion that Charlie was some kind of a cultist or Satanic worship initiate. Further revelations by Poston indicated that Charlie's philosophy drew from sources of Scientology, the Bible, and more recently, vibrations or messages from the lyrics of the Beatles singing group. Charlie had once taught love, flowers and freedom from the Establishment for the Family, but more recently he had developed a bewildering obsession, preaching superstitious lectures on karma and imminent doom. He talked about an impending Armageddon of some sort that prompted him to prepare for the end of western civilization. Poston was so confused by these assertions that he tried to leave the Family several times but told Crockett that Charlie had such an influence on his mind that he didn't know how to leave.

Crockett came to assume that the pair believed Charlie had supernatural powers and had programmed the minds of these young people over a period of time. They told the miner that Charlie planned to come to the desert, and they were emotionally distraught and fearful of the outcome. Crockett pieced together that the cohesiveness of the Family was the result of a blending of drugs, group sex, and mind control. Through Charlie's repetitive preaching of his enigmatic philosophy, it became clear to Crockett that these young people were confused and scared.

The miners fostered in Juanita and Poston an interest in the desert environment, and began to minimize their obvious personal paranoia. Crockett soon had Poston working with him on mining claims, extracting ore samples, and climbing mountains, which resulted in the improvement of his physical condition and distracted him from his involvement with Charlie. Crockett, who believed that Charlie had programmed the young couple into an unwholesome mental state, made an effort to "de-program" them.

Early in July, 1969, another eighteen-year-old, Paul Watkins, came from Los Angeles to the Barker Ranch to visit Wildebush and Poston. He was accompanied by seventeen-year-old Bo Rosenberg, whose real name was Barbara Hoyt. They brought supplies to their friends in the desert. Watkins was somewhat amazed at the transformation in Poston: He was now cheerful, alert, and excited about his experiences with the miners. Poston then introduced Watkins to Crockett, explaining with enthusiasm the activities he and Juanita had shared with him. Bob Berry, Crockett's partner, had gone to Las Vegas for supplies and it was implied that Juanita and Berry had established a relationship.

As Charlie's second in command, Watkins enjoyed the leader's confidence but never completely came under his control. He was Charlie's chief procurer of girls and instilled unity in the Family. Watkins, too, believed Charlie was Jesus Christ returned and was immediately suspicious and disturbed by Crockett's efforts to dissuade his friends from their Family ties. To Watkins, Crockett was a miner, forty-six, short-haired, straight, the epitome of everything Watkins had been programmed to despise. Crockett was the Establishment, a piggy, and so Watkins' initial strategy was to overwhelm Crockett with Charlie's teachings, and to make him aware of Helter Skelter.

Paul Watkins grossly underestimated the character of Paul Crockett. Born in Ada, Oklahoma, of a minister father and a school teacher mother, Crockett left home at 18 and joined the U.S. Air Force to become a navigator. He flew fifty-two combat missions in the South Pacific, and after his combat experience, began asking himself serious questions about life and its purpose. With a parental-inspired thirst for knowledge, he became a reader, not only of technical publications, but also of philosophy, theology, religion, the Bible, history, energy and more. Crockett's study of spiritual disciplines, including scientology, theosophy and the doctrine of the Rosacrucians, gave him the ability to utilize selected precepts for his arguments with Watkins.

Because of his curiosity, he listened to and learned much from Poston and Watkins about the weird predictions of their leader, Charlie. The essence of what they called Helter Skelter was a black revolt. The blacks were going to swarm out over the cities and countryside, killing all the whites except those hiding in the desert. When Helter Skelter came to be fulfilled, they said, the cities would succumb to mass hysteria and the police and the white Establishment, the piggies, wouldn't know what to do. Then the blacks would take over. God was getting ready to pull down the curtain and start all over with his chosen people, Charlie's people.

Charlie's plan was to lead selected whites into the desert, where they would multiply until they reached a population of 144,000. Charlie got this idea from interpreting the Bible passage of Revelation 7, which mentions the twelve tribes of Israel, each numbering 12,000. In Revelations as well as the Hopi Indian legends, Charlie learned about a bottomless pit. According to Charlie, the entrance to this pit was a cave underneath Death Valley that led down to a sea of gold that the Indians knew about. There was a river through the bottomless pit, filled

Death Valley and Panamint Mountains from Furnace Creek Wash. Robert Murphy photo.

with milk and honey, and there was a tree that bore 12 kinds of fruit, a different variety for each month. The place would not be dark, because the walls would glow to furnish light, and it would not be too cold or too hot. There would be warm springs and cold fresh water.

Charlie believed there were people already down there waiting for him. Family members listened attentively to Charlie's sermonizing about this underground sanctuary, a veritable Paradise. Not only did they believe such a place existed, they had spent days searching for the entrance to it in Death Valley in late 1968. Because it was here they intended to wait out Helter Skelter, there was an urgency in their search.

Charlie believed that the English singing group, the Beatles, were the "four angels-leaders, spokesmen and prophets to whom Chapter 9 of Revelation referred: "And he opened the bottomless pit. . .and there came out of the smoke locusts upon the earth; and unto them was given power." Locusts. Beatles. One and the same. "Their faces were as the faces of men, yet they had hair of women." An obvious reference to the long-haired musicians. "Out of the mouths of the four angels issued fire and brimstone." Power came from the mouths of the Beatles in the lyrics of their songs. All of this Charlie proffered to his followers including a reference to Verse 15 which reads, "and the four angels were loosed, which were then prepared for an hour, and a day, and a month, and a year to slay the third part of men"... a third of mankind... the white race.

Charlie believed the Beatles were spokesmen, speaking to him through their songs about the future of mankind. He considered their songs prophecy, especially the "White Album" whose lyrics in his view were interpreted into a message of impending revolution. Almost every song in the album contained a hidden meaning that Charlie interpreted for his Family. To Charlie, "Rocky Raccoon" meant "Coon," or the black man. To him "Happiness is a warm gun" was interpreted to mean the Beatles were telling the blacks to get guns and kill all the whites. The song "Helter Skelter" begins, "When I get to the bottom I go back to the top of the slide, where I stop and I turn and I go for a ride." According to Poston, this referred to the Family emerging from the bottomless pit. However, in England, home of the Beatles, Helter Skelter is another name for a slide in an amusement park. In the song, "Piggies," one can hear background oinks and grunts. To Charlie this was a warning to the piggies, the Establishment and in both songs, "Piggies," and "Revelation 9," there is an odd chord that Charlie said is a machine gun firing, people dying and screaming. The Beatles are telling people what is going to happen. There was also a man's voice saying, "Rise," which Charlie interpreted to mean that now was the time to rise and start it all.

According to Charlie, now was the time. He saw all the signs in the world around him. Blacks were rioting and killing whites, and open revolution was occurring, with blacks winning and taking over. There were atrocities- stabbings, killing, mutilation of bodies, the smearing of blood on walls, and the writing of "pig" on the walls in the victims' own blood. Charlie believed that all would be killed except him and his Family, who had taken refuge in the bottomless pit in Death Valley. The Family, after having grown to 144,000 as predicted in the Bible, a pure, white and master race, would emerge from the bottomless pit. The blacks wouldn't know what to do with the arisen Christ's power and Charlie would take over. It would be Charlie's world. He had said there will be "no one but us and the black servants."

Paul Watkins' efforts to convince Paul Crockett of the coming all-out war, of his loyalty and belief in Charlie, were received with indifference. Crockett in a sincere manner told young Watkins that his belief in Helter Skelter was sheer fantasy; it was just in their heads. If they thought and believed that's what was going to happen and continued to believe in it, that's what they'd get. To Crockett, the whole idea was preposterous.

After several conversations in which Crockett inferred that Watkins' mental state was unstable, the young man became bewildered. Bob Berry returned from Las Vegas and his sexual relationship with the liberated Juanita was clear, and this also puzzled Watkins. For the first time, Watkins became aware that Crockett had a great influence on the people around him. Poston and Wildebush had both told Crockett that they wanted to be liberated from the Family. He explained his own philosophy and attempted daily to de-program the two young people.

Watkins soon learned that Crockett's logic was much more understandable than Charlie's. Poston told Watkins that Crockett had put up a psychic barrier on Goler Wash to keep Charlie out. Three times the Family had tried to leave Los Angeles for Death Valley, and each time the attempt had failed. Watkins was convinced that Helter Skelter was questionable. Unknown to those at the Barker Ranch, he was most disturbed by Charlie's change from love and flowers to what seemed more like an obsession with death. Watkins, somewhat bewildered after three days at Barker Ranch, departed with Bo Rosenberg for the old Spahn Movie Ranch in the Los Angeles area, where the Family was staying.

A day or two later, Watkins returned to the Barker Ranch, alone and greatly disturbed by what he had learned at Spahn Ranch. The whole Family was talking about killing and death. Charlie told him in confidence, "We are going to have to show Blackie how to do it." Watkins wasn't sure of his freedom from Charlie, but he wanted to stay at the Barker Ranch for a while.

Paul Watkins and Brooks Poston appeared to have found a companion in Paul Crockett. There was a change in the atmosphere around the Barker Ranch. Crockett, accustomed to the hard work associated with his prospecting, did not approve of the use of drugs. The diversion of prospecting, scouring the desert, and different topics of conversation were a departure from the youths' former preoccupation with Charlie's weird and fatal predictions.

Moreover, Juanita Wildebush and Bob Berry were obviously in love and were enthusiastic with the direction Crockett provided. There was even a small garden that Juanita watered and cultivated, which brought them rewards for the dinner table. There were frequent hiking trips by Crockett's group into the mountains and occasional trips to Shoshone for supplies.

Deputy Ward was puzzled by Crockett's association with the hippies. One day in August he followed them out of town and pulled them over. Ward was still concerned about the marijuana incidents and confronted the group about being in town for the purpose of pushing pot. Crockett assured Ward that such considerations were in the past and would not happen again. Ward, skeptical, left them with the understanding he would be watching their travels around town.

In early August, Bob Berry and Juanita Wildebush left Barker Ranch, were reportedly married in Las Vegas, and moved on to Arizona. In a rather harmonious atmosphere, Crockett, Watkins, and Poston continued their mining pursuits in Goler Wash.

·5·
A Deluded Prophet in the Desert

There is no doubt that the man who led the retreat to the desert in revamped dune buggies had a special power over his young followers. He could silence them with a nod of his head, or he could terrorize them into sexual or antisocial acts by a growl as a command. The life of Charles Manson is a testimony to the lost lives of neglected and unwanted children. The power of his delusion reflects the corruption of an unrooted life.

By the time Charlie was thirty-two years old, he had spent more than half his life in confining institutions. He was born November 12, 1934, in Cincinnati, the illegitimate son of sixteen-year-old Kathleen Maddox. He would later state that his mother was a teen-age prostitute, but relatives said she was merely an uncontrolled teen-ager who ran around a lot and got into trouble. She lived with a succession of men, including an older man, William Manson, whom she married just long enough to provide a name for her child.

But just who Charlie's father was remains in doubt. In 1936, Kathleen filed suit for support against a "Colonel Scott," a resident of Ashland, Kentucky. The court awarded her a judgment of $25, plus $5 a month for the support of "Charles Milles Manson." Colonel Scott failed to honor the judgment and years later Kathleen attempted to attach his wages. His reported death in 1954 has not been verified. Charlie later stated that he had never met his father.

The youngster bounced around from obliging neighbors to his grandmother or maternal aunt while his mother disappeared for days or weeks at a time. Most of his early years were spent in West Virginia, Kentucky, or Ohio. In 1939 Kathleen and her brother Luther robbed a Charleston, West Virginia, service station and were sentenced to prison for five years. While his mother was in prison, Manson lived with an aunt and uncle in West Virginia. They had marital problems until they became interested in religion and became fanatics. Now, Charlie was confronted by an aunt who thought all pleasures sinful, but gave him love, where before he had had a permissive mother who let him do anything he wanted as long as he did not bother her. Obviously, it was a bewildering experience.

Paroled in 1942, Kathleen reclaimed Charlie, then eight years old. For the next several years, mother and son lived in sleazy hotel rooms and Charlie met a succession of "uncles," most of whom, like his mother, drank heavily. In 1947 she tried to put him in a foster home. The court sent him to Gibault School for Boys, a caretaking institution in Terre Haute, Indiana. School records indicate he made a poor adjustment and that at his best his attitude toward school was only fair. He had a tendency toward moodiness and a persecution complex. After ten months, he ran away to rejoin his mother.

She didn't want him, and he ran away again. He burglarized a grocery store for enough money to rent a room, then broke into several businesses, stealing a number of items, including a bicycle. He was caught during a burglary and placed in a juvenile center in Indianapolis. He escaped the next day. When he was again in custody, the court erroneously was informed that Charlie was Catholic and through a local priest, arrangements were made to have him accepted at Father Flanigan's Boys Town in Nebraska.

Four days after his arrival, he and another boy stole a car and fled to his friend's uncle in Peoria, Illinois. They committed two armed robberies en route, one at a grocery store and the other at a gambling casino. At the age of thirteen, Charlie was fully matured in crime, graduating from non-violence to violence.

A week after arriving in Peoria, the pair broke into a grocery store and stole $1,500, for which the uncle gave them $150. A repeat performance brought apprehension again, and this time Manson went to the Indiana School for Boys at Plainfield, where he ran away eighteen times in three years. According to his teachers, he trusted no one and "did good work for those from whom he figured he could obtain something."

In February of, 1951, Charlie and two other fifteen-year-olds escaped and headed for California. They stole cars and burglarized gas stations along the way, probably as many as 20, Manson related later. Outside of Beaver, Utah, they ran into a road-block set up for robbery suspects.

In taking a stolen car across state lines, the youths had violated the federal Dyer Act and Charlie was confined to the National Training School for Boys in Washington, D.C. On arrival he was given a battery of tests, and though he had completed four years of school, he remained illiterate. His I.Q. was 109. His case worker reported that he was a sixteen-year-old boy who had had an unfavorable family life, if it could be called a family at all, and he was aggressively anti-social.

After three months, his record showed that he had become an

institutional politician, one who did only enough work to get by, was restless and moody and spent his time entertaining friends. The record states that he was a boy who was a very emotionally upset youth who was definitely in need of psychiatric help.

A psychiatrist examined Charlie and noted that he had a marked degree of rejection, instability, and psychic trauma in his background. His sense of inferiority in relation to his mother was so pronounced, Block said, that he constantly felt it was necessary to suppress any thoughts about her. Because of his diminutive stature, his illegitimacy, and lack of parental love, he was constantly striving for status with other boys.

For three months, the doctor gave Charlie individual psychotherapy, and it may be presumed that he worked his "spell" on the doctor. In his October report, Block stated that he was convinced that what Manson most required were experiences to build his self confidence; in short, he needed to be trusted. The doctor recommended a transfer. Charlie had conned his first psychiatrist. Although school authorities considered that at best he was a calculated risk, on October 24 he was transferred to Natural Bridge Honor Camp, a minimum-security institution of Charlie's own choosing.

In November he turned seventeen. Shortly thereafter he was visited by an aunt who offered to supply a home and employment for him. He was due for a parole hearing in February of 1952, and with his aunt's offer, his chances for parole looked good. Instead, less than a month before the hearing, Charlie took a razor blade and held it against another boy's throat while he sodomized him.

A short time later he was transferred to the Federal Reformatory at Petersburg, Virginia, where he was considered "dangerous" and shouldn't have been trusted across the street. Within a few months he had committed eight disciplinary offenses, three involving homosexual acts. His progress report, if it could be called that, stated that Charlie had definite homosexual and aggressive tendencies. He was classified as safe only under supervision and for his protection as well as that of others, he was transferred to a more secure institution, the Federal Reformatory at Chillicothe, Ohio, September 22, 1952.

Chillicothe files reported that Charlie associated with troublemakers, seemed to be the unpredictable type of inmate who required supervision both at work and in quarters, and in spite of his age was criminally sophisticated. He was regarded as grossly unsuited for retention in an open reformatory such as Chillicothe.

Then suddenly he changed. For the rest of the year he had no serious disciplinary offenses. An October report noted that he had shown remarkable improvement in his general attitude and cooperation with officers and was also taking an active interest in the educational program. January 1, 1954, he was given a meritorious service award and on May 8 of that year was granted a parole. He was nineteen.

A condition of his parole was that Charlie live with an uncle and aunt in nearby McMechen, West Virginia, and there he rejoined his mother who had moved to nearby Wheeling. Shortly after his release he met a seventeen-year-old McMechen girl, Rosalie Jean Willis, an employee of a local hospital. They were married in January of 1955. Manson worked as a service station helper and parking lot attendant. He had a fondness for automobiles and later admitting stealing six, crossing state lines. One stolen in Wheeling he abandoned in Fort Lauderdale, Florida, and in another, accompanied by his now pregnant wife, he drove from Bridgeport, Ohio, to Los Angeles, but was arrested less than three months later, admitting to both Dyer Act violations. He gave the court an impassioned plea concerning his need for psychiatric treatment and was examined October 26, 1955. He told the psychiatrist that he had been sent to an institution for being mean to his mother, and said that he now had a good wife who was going to have a baby. The doctor was of the opinion that he had spent nine years on probation, but the incentive of a wife might straighten him out. He recommended the court consider probation with supervision and on November 5, 1955, the court gave Manson five years probation.

The Florida charge remained and although chances were excellent that Charlie might receive probation, he skipped. He was picked up March 14, 1956, in Indianapolis on a warrant and returned to Los Angeles, where his probation was revoked. He was sentenced to three years at Terminal Island, San Pedro, and by the time his son, Charles Manson, Jr., was born, he was behind bars.

Rosalie moved in with his mother, now living in Los Angeles, and during his first year at Terminal Island visited him every week. Manson's work habits varied from poor to good as noted in his March 1957 progress report. However, at the time of his parole hearing, his work performance had jumped from good to excellent. His parole hearing was set for April 22.

In March, Rosalie's visits ceased. She was living with another man. In early April, he was transferred to a Coast Guard unit under minimal security. He was indicted for attempted escape with an automobile, five years were tacked onto his probation, and his parole request was denied.

Rosalie filed for divorce, which became final in 1958. She retained custody of young Charles, remarried, and had no further contact with Manson or his mother.

In April 1958 Charlie's progress was reported as "sporadic" and his behavior as "erratic and moody." Later he was said to be improving but future adjustment was difficult to predict. Yet, in September of 1958 he was released on five years parole. By November, he was pimping for a known procurer in Malibu. When his parole officer called him on it, he denied pimping and said he was no longer associated with his Malibu friend. On May 1, 1959, he was arrested for attempting to pass a U.S. Treasury check in Los Angeles. He had stolen it from a mail box. In mid-June, an attractive nineteen-year-old girl named Leona called his parole officer and reported she was pregnant by Charlie. The parole officer was skeptical and wanted to see a medical report. He also began checking on her background.

Manson's luck held and with the aid of an attorney he agreed to plead guilty to forging the check if the mail theft was dropped. The judge ordered a psychiatric examination. Manson appeared in court September 29, 1959. The psychiatrist, the U.S. Attorney's Office and the probation department all recommended against probation. Leona was there also and made a tearful plea on Manson's behalf, telling the court they were deeply in love and that she would marry Charlie if he were free. Not only had Leona lied about being pregnant, she had an arrest record as a prostitute under the name of Candy Stevens. Moved by her tears, the judge gave the defendant a ten-year suspended sentence and Manson was back on the street.

By December he had been arrested by Los Angeles police for grand theft auto and use of stolen credit cards, but both charges were dismissed for lack of evidence. That month he took Leona and a girl named Elizabeth to Lordburg, New Mexico, for the purpose of prostitution, violating the federal Mann Act. Questioned and released, he married Leona, possibly to prevent her from testifying against him. He remained free through January while the FBI checked the New Mexico offense.

Manson was not idle. Befriending a girl from Detroit who had fallen for a fraudulent airline stewardess school in a magazine advertisement in Los Angeles, Charlie became the president of a phony company, Three Star Enterprises, Night Club, Radio and TV Promotions, apparently financed liberally by Mary Jo. She was staying in an apartment with a friend, Rita. Manson drugged and raped Rita and got Mary Jo pregnant. It was a Fallopian pregnancy from which she nearly died.

Manson skipped and on April 28, he was indicted on the Mann Act charge. Arrested in Laredo, Texas, he was brought back to Los Angeles. Leona, the girl who had cried in court, was arrested in Laredo for prostitution. She had previously been picked up in Beverly Hills for a similar offense. In June, 1960, the court ruled that Charlie had violated the terms of his probation and ordered him back to prison to serve out his ten-year term. He sat in the Los Angeles jail for a year while his appeal was processed. It was denied and in July, 1961, he went to the U.S. Penitentiary at McNeil Island, Washington. He was twenty-six.

Charlie claimed his religion was Scientology, an outgrowth of fiction writer L. Ron Hubbard's Dianetics. Manson's teacher was another convict, Lanier Rayner, who broke away from Scientology to form his own group. He was apprehended in a shotgun holdup and sent to McNeil Island. Supposedly Charlie had 150 "processing" sessions with Rayner, but his interest in Scientology lasted only as long as his enthusiasm. He borrowed from it and adapted its practice methods to his own version, retaining a number of related phrases, "cease to exist," "mock up," and "come to now." He would later develop his own expressions to program young minds, such a "you are me and I am you," "fear is beautiful," and "helter skelter."

Charlie remained interested in Scientology. When his annual report was written in September his evaluator wrote: "Manson is making progress for the first time in his life. He has become somewhat of a fanatic at practicing the guitar." In June, 1966, he was returned to Terminal Island for release processing.

His August, 1966, evaluation was pessimistic. "He has a pattern of criminal behavior that dates to his teen years. This pattern is one of instability whether in a free society or a structured institutional community. Little can be expected in the way of change in his attitude, behavior or mode of conduct. He has come to worship his guitar and music. He has no plans for release as he says he has no place to go."

Yet on March 21, 1967, Charles Manson was out of prison and back on the streets of Los Angeles.

•6•
Assembling The Family

What better place in 1967 could a man who was enraptured with his guitar and its songs, his prison sophistication, and his compulsion to influence girls go than to ultra-liberal Berkeley, California? He went there to impress people as a wandering minstrel singer. One spring day while sitting and singing in an open air mall on the University of California campus, this degenerate graduate of the toughest of the nation's reformatories and prisons met Mary Brunner, an assistant librarian for the University. She was twenty-three, a recent graduate of the University of Wisconsin, and unattractive. Manson apparently thought she was worth cultivating and subsequently moved into her apartment. There were other girls that Manson moved in and out of her apartment, but Mary was tolerant. In that summer of 1967, Manson roamed up and down the coast of California and received permission from his parole officer to leave the state on occasion.

In Venice, he picked up a young red-head, Lynette Fromme, also known as Elizabeth Elaine Williamson, who had been removed from her father's house after a series of quarrels. In San Francisco, Manson, Brunner, and Fromme took up residence near Haight Street, where acid-dropping was a daily part of their lives. Charlie, a grubby ex-con with a guitar, was in his element, scrounging for young girls with his mysticism and guru, cultist babble.

In September, 1967, Manson, Fromme and Brunner visited a former jail inmate in Manhattan Beach. Visiting there was Patricia Krenwinkle, known in the Family as Katie, and Marnie Reaves, eighteen, a lonely searching girl from Inglewood. Marnie was a Bible freak who later completely immersed herself in the acid religion of Manson. Patricia had been a process clerk for an insurance company. Her father would recall that Patricia left her apartment, her job, and her car, not even picking up her pay check to join Charlie, convinced that he was some sort of a hypnotist. Among her assets were a telephone credit card and a Chevron credit card, whose obligations her loving father continued to pay.

In September, 1967, the group drove to Oregon in a Volkswagen microbus that Charlie had acquired from Dean Morehouse, a minister in San Jose. He had a fourteen-year-old daughter, Ruth Ann, who became the Family's Ouisch, ripe and ready for Manson's cultivation. On the trip north, the growing Family met Bruce Davis, a dropout from the University of Tennessee and a transient undergrounder. He would became a dedicated male follower of Charlie.

The Family had grown too large for the microbus, so in Sacramento they traded the microbus in as a down payment on an old yellow school bus. Rear seats were removed to create a living area and the bus became their traveling home. In early November, Manson went to San Francisco where he met Susan Atkins at an apartment on Lime Street. She was a rather attractive nineteen-year-old from San Jose. There had been a lot of fighting and drinking in her home and her mother had died of cancer when Susan was thirteen. At sixteen she dropped out of school and went San Francisco, where she worked at menial jobs and tried drugs. On September 12, 1966, she was arrested in Oregon along with two ex-con boyfriends on stolen auto and armed robbery charges. After three months in jail she was placed on probation and returned to San Francisco to resume a career as waitress and topless dancer.

Susan expanded her use of LSD, experimented with satanic worship, and had a number of male friends. She then met Charlie and reportedly had the most gratifying love experience of her nineteen years. Manson went back to Sacramento, picked up the newly-decorated school bus, enlisted Susan as a new member and headed for Los Angeles, stopping to pick up Ouisch in San Jose. Three days later an outraged Rev. Morehouse found his daughter in Los Angeles. After socializing with Charlie and possibly being pacified with drugs, he returned to San Jose, somewhat convinced his daughter was in good hands.

On November 12, 1967, Manson was thirty-three.

The first trip as a family into the Mohave Desert was possibly made in November of 1967. They visited Owens Valley, and probably Ridgecrest and Trona. After a brief return to Los Angeles, the Family was off to Santa Barbara and San Francisco, then back in the desert, stopping in and around Death Valley and visiting in Las Vegas before proceeding across Arizona and New Mexico to Texas. The bus, with a coat of black paint, was back in Los Angeles on December 14, 1967.

The Family was to establish roots in Los Angeles, first in an ancient two-story house on Topanga Canyon Lane that became a "scrounge lounge" for the Family. It was called the "Spiral Staircase" because of its interior second floor access. Here the Family first met Robert K. Beausoleil, a twenty-year-old small-time actor and musician, with an interest in devil worship and magic. Beausoleil was a friend of Gary Hinman, a music teacher. He and a girlfriend lived in Hinman's small hillside home at 946 Old Topanga Canyon Road. Hinman permitted people in transit to use his home, including members of the Family, who ultimately teamed up with Beausoleil to murder their host.

Another convert was Diane Lake, also known as Diane Bluestein. At the age of thirteen, Diane was a member of the Hog Farm Commune in Los Angeles and was sophisticated in group sex and LSD. Her parents permitted her to travel with the Family, although later her mother would try to reclaim her at Spahn Ranch. Diane acquired the nickname of Snake, presumably from ophidian movements in her sexual engagements.

Strange doors opened to the strange Family as others moved in and out of the house. A variety of pursuits gave them sustenance. Panhandling from either friends or strangers was favored. At times the girls worked at odd jobs or made garbage runs on the local supermarket. Manson, an established con artist, hit rich residential areas with trumped up causes. Occasionally the Family played for money in sleazy joints, usually of short duration because the group was too far out and undependable. Stolen credit cards, shoplifting and pushing drugs were commonly used to keep their enterprise afloat.

In February of 1968, the Family moved in with Robert Beausoleil at his deteriorated home in Topanga Canyon. About this time the Family recruited Nancy Laura Pitman, alias Brenda McCann, of Malibu, and Madaline Joan Cottage, alias Linda Baldwin, whom the Family knew as Little Patty. About this time Yellerstone, Ella Jo Bailey, also joined up.

Charlie's friend, Phil Kaufman, was released from prison in March. Kaufman had a friend, Harold True, who lived in a fine home at 3267 Waverly Drive, near the Silver Lake area of Los Angeles. Before True moved out of this house, he was introduced to Charlie and Family members through Kaufman. Manson visited the house during the summer, sleeping there on at least two occasions. Next door was a home that would be purchased by Leno and Rosemary LaBianca in November of 1968.

On April 1, 1968, a son, Valentine Michael Manson, was born to Mary Brunner, who was attended at the birth by only a few Family friends in a new location, a shacky place on Summit Trail off Topanga Canyon. About this time arrived Sandra Good, twenty, daughter of a San Diego Stockbroker. She had been in on the growth of Haight-Ashbury and came seeking Charlie's acid sexual commune. Her skill at coaxing money from her well-to-do father kept her in good standing with Manson.

In early March a seventeen-year-old dropout named Paul Watkins came seeking a friend at Summit Trail. Instead, he found naked women and Charles Manson. That night Watkins witnessed and participated in group sexual psychodramas, with musical accompaniment and LSD appetizers.

In April, 1968, the Family, now twenty in number, moved to Leo Carillo State Park, setting up tents. Bruce Davis, whom the Family had encountered a few months before, joined and became an avid member. The Family moved up the coast and were continually plagued by arrests for drugs, felonious accounts, and false identification in one form or another. On release from jail they headed for the old Spahn Movie Ranch near Chatsworth, then traveled north to Mendocino County and back to Los Angeles.

About this time they moved into the luxurious home of Dennis Wilson, member of the successful musical group, the Beach Boys. It was reported that Wilson had earlier picked up, in Malibu, a couple of members of the Family, Ella Jo Bailey and Patricia Krenwinkle, and took them home with him where they spent a couple of hours talking about Charlie.

Wilson had a recording session one night and did not return to his home until about 3:00 a.m., when he was confronted by Charlie. He thought he was about to be a victim of robbery or worse. Wilson was ushered into his own house and confronted by more than a dozen uninvited guests, mostly naked girls.

Wilson hosted them in varying numbers for several months. He estimated the experience cost him about $100,000. Charlie constantly hit him up for money, Clem demolished his Ferrari, and the Family appropriated his wardrobe and everything else of value. In what he referred to as probably "the largest gonorrhea bill in history," he took the whole Family several times to his own physician for pencillin shots. Wilson gave Charlie nine or ten Beach Boy gold records. He obviously found something attractive about the Family lifestyle, except the expense.

Manson haunted successful rock musicians and related industries on Sunset Boulevard, living in Wilson's Pacific Palisades home with excellent opportunities to impress Wilson's associates toward recognition of Family members as musicians and recording artists. He met Greg Jackson, a song writer and colleague of Terry Melcher, Doris Day's son, who managed various music publishing and TV enterprises. These people were not appreciably impressed.

Melcher lived at 10050 Cielo Drive, the home owned by Rudi Altobelli, a Hollywood talent manager. Melcher brushed Manson aside, and Charlie was so upset that he later threatened to cut and bury Melcher. Melcher later moved into his mother's Malibu Beach home and assigned his unexpired lease to Roman Polanski and his actress wife on February 12, 1969. On August 9, 1969, Family members would brutally murder Sharon Tate and four other prominent personalities at 10050 Cielo Drive.

While the Family was associated with Dennis Wilson, a seventeen-year-old Texan named Brooks Poston became infatuated with Manson's religious philosophy and stayed.

Possibly Charlie's greatest work in diabolical magic was the transformation of nineteen-year-old Charles Denton Watson, known as Tex. He, with a partner, had a wig shop in Beverly Hills. He was clean-cut, with a mod look. In Texas, he has been a popular high school athlete and college dropout. With dope and Satanic fever, the Family nearly erased his good looks and his mind. Tex would complain later that he actually thought he was Charles Manson.

Pressures on Dennis Wilson became intolerable, and he moved to a house on the beach. His business manager had the Family moved from his Sunset Boulevard property. The Family moved back to the Spahn Ranch. Eighteen-year-old Clem Tufts, whose true name was Steve Grogan, had been living with a hippie group at the rear of the Spahn Ranch and readily joined the Family. His criminal record included drug use and possession, shoplifting, grand theft, prowling, child molesting and indecent exposure. Evaluations indicated that his sanity was marginal, and that he was really "spaced out."

Prior to the move back to Spahn Ranch, Bobby Beausoleil was traveling in northern California with his own wandering Family. After some internal strife one of the members, Gypsy, Catherine Share, left for Spahn Ranch. Born in Paris in 1942 of Hungarian-German Jewish parents who were in the French underground during the war and committed suicide, Gypsy was adopted and brought to the United States at the age of eight. She was graduated from Hollywood High School, attended college for three years, married and was divorced. She was a musician and had a beautiful singing voice. She had bit parts in movies when she first met Beausoleil and then Charlie who convinced her his dogma was ordained.

From the Beausoleil group also came Leslie Van Houten, eighteen. Her parents separated when she was fourteen and that same year, she became pregnant, had an abortion and began taking LSD acid regularly. She ran away to Haight-Ashbury, became frightened, finished high school and took a year of secretarial training. She spent eight months in training as a novitiate nun, dropped out, went back to drugs and ended up in a commune in northern California with Bobby Beausoleil.

Juan Flynn, a tall Irish-Panamanian, worked at Spahn Ranch and was admired by Manson. He was invited to take part in the acid-love orgies, but never really let Charlie dominate his mind.

In late summer, 1968, Cathie Gillies, also known as Patty Sue Jardin, joined the family at Spahn ranch. Her grandmother owned Myers Ranch in Death Valley. She heavily used drugs and had associated with hippie and motorcycle gangs. Her grandparents, Bill and Barbara Myers, had been teachers who visited Death Valley in the early 1930s, appreciated the place, and bought a mining claim on Goler Wash so their children could enjoy the natural values of the area. They used the ranch as a base of recreation and exploration in the desert. They bought the Wildrose Canyon Resort and operated it from 1951 to 1957 when they moved back to the San Joaquin Valley but kept title to the Goler Wash Ranch, which their granddaughter had visited, although she had not lived there.

From his experience in Death Valley, Charlie decided dune buggies were the vehicle for his Family's mobility. he first bought two rail-job buggies but later resorted to stealing VW bugs, stripping them, and converting them to dune buggies. Still later he stole new units off sales lots and stashed them in hidden locations.

Charlie recruited an ex-con friend, William Joseph Vance, true name David Lee Hamic, who made arrangements for some of the girls to work as topless dancers in San Fernando Valley clubs. Vance could steal just about anything Charlie wanted. Others helped to prepare for Helter Skelter by stealing motor parts, camping gear, tents, food supplies—anything that was needed. Bikers who helped in this knew little of Charlie's plans but worked in exchange for easy sex and good drugs.

May 27, 1969, Darwin Orell Scott was found hacked to death in his Ashland, Kentucky, apartment. He was stabbed nineteen times and pinned to the floor with a butcher knife. Scott was the brother of Colonel Scott, the man alleged to be Charlie's father. In the spring of 1969, a motorcycle-riding guru who called himself "Preacher" appeared in Ashland with several female followers. He was generous with LSD to local teenagers and attempted to set up a commune in a ramshackle farmhouse. In April, irate citizens burned down the house and drove off the hippies. Some would later claim that Preacher and Charlie were one and the same. Evidence at hand documented that Manson was in California the day of Scott's murder; however, on May 22, he telephoned his parole officer for permission to accompany the Beach Boys to Texas. Permission was withheld, pending certification that Charlie was employed by the Beach Boys.

In a letter dated May 27, he notified his parole officer that he had moved from Death Valley back to Spahn Ranch. The parole officer's control over Charlie must have been minimal because he did not talk with him again until June 18. He received the supposed May 27 letter June 3, seven days after it was supposedly written. Manson could have been using the letter as an alibi, or he had sent one of his killers to murder Scott.

On July 4, 1969, Linda Kasabian, nineteen, and her two-year-old daughter arrived at Spahn ranch to join the Family. She came from a broken home and had already had two unsuccessful marriages, the second to a young hippie, Robert Kasabian. Being pregnant, she had recently come from New Hampshire to Los Angeles to attempt a reconciliation. Failing in that, she joined the Family. No novice to the ways of the world, Linda had been on her own since age sixteen. She had lived in communes from Taos to Seattle, had experienced Haight-Ashbury and was into drugs and easy sex. She fell under Charlie's spell for a time. A little over a month after she joined the Family, he sent her to kill, but she refused to follow his command.

After witnessing two nights of murder, she escaped to Taos, returning to reclaim her daughter, Tanya, from a social worker. She hitch-hiked to her father in Miami, Florida, and then to her mother's home in New Hampshire. She was located there and voluntarily returned to Los Angeles and served as a key witness for the prosecution in the Tate-LaBianca murder trials.

Two youths from Ohio, John Philip Haught, also known as Christopher Jesus and Zero, and Kenneth Richard Brown, who became Scotty Davis, and a third from Oklahoma, Lawrence Charles Bailey, also known as Larry Jones, became part of the Family. Scotty, Zero, Vance and Vern Plumlee became the theft squad that roamed Los Angeles, robbing service stations, burglarizing shops and residences, forging stolen credit cars and stealing vehicles.

On July 1, 1969, Tex Watson accompanied a black man and a young woman to El Monte where the black man, Bernard Crowe, gave Watson $2,400 with which to buy dope. Watson went into a house to make the purchase and skipped out the back door, leaving Crowe and the woman to wait in the car.

Crowe, extremely irate, phoned Charlie and threatened to come to the Spahn Ranch and shoot it up. Manson is said to have told him that he would go instead to Crowe's place. Armed with his .22-caliber Buntline revolver, Charlie, accompanied by T. J. Walleman, went to visit Crowe.

As Charlie entered the residence, he placed the revolver on a table and offered to let Crowe use the gun to kill him. Crowe said he did not want to harm Charlie, only those who burned him. Charlie made a jovial remark, picked up the revolver and prepared to leave. T. J. and two of Crowe's friends were in the room. Crowe stood up and is said to have said, "Are you going to shoot me?" and put his hand on his abdomen. Charlie, about eight feet away, pointed the gun and pulled the trigger—click. Charlie was quick to remark, "How could I kill you with an empty gun?" The trigger clicked a second time and then there was a shot. Crowe fell to the floor clutching his abdomen. Charlie is reported to have turned to one of Crowe's friends, admiring his leather shirt. The man quickly took it off and handed it to Charlie.

Manson and Walleman went back to the ranch. The next day T. J. left, saying he wanted nothing to do with "snuffing people." Crowe did not die. He was operated on at the USC hospital and survived to be incarcerated with Charlie in the spring of 1970.

The day after the shooting there was panic at the ranch. Someone reportedly called Charlie and told him they had dumped Crowe's body in a park. Fear of retaliation possessed the Family. Possibly Charlie considered that he might be the first white victim of Helter Skelter. Night foot patrols were established and armed guards were posted on the roofs of buildings, evidently awaiting the arrival of Black Panthers.

Early in the morning of July 17, 1969, Mark Walts, sixteen, left his home in Chatsworth and hitchhiked to Santa Monica pier to go fishing. His fishing pole was found on the pier, and his body was discovered a day later off Topanga Canyon Boulevard a short distance from Mulholland. He had been severely beaten and bruised about the head and shot three times in the chest with a .22-caliber weapon. Walts was not a Spahn Ranch hand or a Family member, although he did hang around the ranch. Sheriff's officers checked out the ranch but could find no evidence to link anyone there with the killing. Walts' older brother called the ranch to tell Charlie, "I know you done my brother in. I'm going to come down there and kill you." He did not follow through with the threat, but he obviously felt Manson was responsible.

The Family was now established to Charlie's liking and training, for the ultimate Helter Skelter had begun. Killing had become easy for the Mansonites. Free, uninhibited group sex, plenty of the most vicious kind of mind-altering drugs, and a leader born and reared in violence were to make his Satanic cult capable of the brutal, seemingly unmotivated murders that were to shock Southern California.

·7·

The Brutal
Los Angeles
Murders

Late in the afternoon of July 31, 1969, a call was made to the Los Angeles sheriff's homicide office on the third floor of the Hall of Justice in downtown Los Angeles about the death of a man, possibly a murder victim or a suicide. The two officers on duty were Sgt. Paul Whitely and Deputy Charles Guenther. It was near the end of their day shift, but they decided to drive out to Topanga Canyon and check out the possibility of crime. From the state of the body and the general scene, they believed it was murder, committed a few days earlier.

For most of three days inside the residence, the officers sifted through personal belongings and determined that the victim was Gary Hinman, a part-time music teacher.

On the morning of August 6, a California Highway Patrol car stopped behind a Fiat parked along Highway 101 near San Luis Obispo. The officer awakened a man who was asleep in a sleeping bag in the rear seat. The individual had no driver's license and gave the name of Robert Beausoleil. Calling in the license number, the officer was informed that the car was reported stolen. He took Beausoleil to the local CHP station and was informed there was an all-points bulletin alert that the car be impounded and the occupants held in connection with Hinman's death.

The Fiat was locked for security of evidence and towed into custody in San Luis Obispo. That same day, Whitely and Guenther, accompanied by a fingerprint expert, arrived in San Luis Obispo to interrogate Beausoleil. He talked little at first, but finally admitted he had been to Hinman's house with two women. The next day he was brought to Los Angles and booked as a homicide suspect. The officers learned that Beausoleil had a girlfriend named Kitty Lutesinger whose parents lived in Northridge, California. The two deputies drove to Northridge to talk to Mrs. Lutesinger. She revealed that her problem daughter had run away several times. When the officers discovered her daughter was only seventeen, they urged Mrs. Lutesinger to file appropriate notice with authorities; her daughter was a juvenile runaway. Whitely left her his identification card with a phone number to call in case she learned of her daughter's location.

On August 10, while autopsies were in progress on the five victims brutally murdered at the home of Sharon Tate, Sergeants Whitely and Guenther of the Los Angeles Sheriff's Department approached Sergeant Buckles, a Los Angeles Police Department detective assigned to the Tate murders, and told him something curious.

On July 31, they had gone to 964 Topanga Road in Malibu to investigate a possible homicide. They found the body of Gary Hinman, a 34-year-old music teacher. He had been stabbed to death in exactly the same way as the Tate killings, and a message had been left at the scene. On a wall not far from Hinman's body were the words, "political piggy," printed in the victim's own blood.

Whitely also told Buckles they had arrested in connection with the murder, Robert "Bobby" Beausoleil, a young musician. That arrest occurred August 6, and Beausoleil was in custody at the time of the Tate homicides. Whitely also thought it was very possible Beausoleil was not the only one involved in the Hinman murder.

Beausoleil had been friendly with a bunch of hippies who lived on an old movie ranch near the Los Angeles suburb of Chatsworth. He was known to have stayed there on occasion. Buckles apparently lost interest when Whitely mentioned hippies. He told the sheriff's men that the LAPD's investigation had already revealed what was behind the murders.

"It is a retaliation concerning a big dope transaction," he said.

Whitely again emphasized the similarities. The death mode was the same and in both instances a message had been left, both printed in the victim's own blood. In both cases the word "pig" appeared. The odds against the similarities were astronomical but Buckles and the LAPD told Whitely and Guenther, "If you don't hear from us in a week or two, that means we're onto something else."

Whitely and Guenther's intuition had been right on target. For at the old Spahn Ranch during the hot evening of Friday, August 8, 1969, Charlie Manson had evidently made plans to shock the world and to begin Helter Skelter with his own bizarre methods. He is reported to have instructed Susan Atkins, Linda Kasabian, and Patricia Krenwinkel to get extra dark clothing and knives. Linda was given her driver's license and thought they were going on another creepy crawly excursion. They were joined by Charles "Tex" Watson who had evidently received instructions from Charlie. They departed in Johnny

Swartz's old yellow and white 1959 Ford sedan. In the car was a pair of red-handled bolt cutters, a forty-three foot length of three-strand nylon rope, and a .22-caliber revolver. Tex also had one of the double-edged bayonets stowed away. While enroute he told the girls that they were going to 10050 Cielo Drive off Benedict Canyon in the Hollywood Hills. This secluded location was Terry Melcher's former place, but he no longer lived there. The plan was to go there and kill whoever was there, possibly take their money, and to definitely leave a sign.

Sharon Tate, age 25, and her husband, controversial movie director, Roman Polanski, had taken over Terry Melcher's unexpired lease on the Cielo Drive palatial residence on February 12, 1969. Sharon had had a long struggle in the movie industry, having bit parts in the TV series "The Beverly Hillbillies," "Petticoat Junction," and two Ranshoff films, "The Americanization of Emily," and "The Sandpiper." Through Ranshoff she was cast in "Eye of the Devil" starring David Niven and Deborah Kerr. The film was made in London and there, in the summer of 1966, she met Roman Polanski.

Roman was, at the time, thirty-three, and one of Europe's leading movie directors. Born in Paris, his father was a Russian Jew, his mother Polish of Russian stock. From Poland's war-torn cities, his parents in a concentration camp, young Polanski escaped to live with friends until the war ended. After the war he attended the Polish National Film Academy in Lodz. In the following years he made a number of short films, one in which a Polish friend, Voytek Frykowski, played a part. A later feature-length film, "Knife in the Water," won the Critics Award at the Venice Film Festival. In 1965, he made his first film in English, exploiting violence as the theme. Sharon had a part in one of his films and after a rather lengthy courtship they became lovers. Later Paramount asked Polanski to do the film version of Ira Levin's novel, "Rosemary's Baby." The film was completed in late 1967 and to the surprise of Roman's friends, he and Sharon were married on January 20, 1968, in London. That same month the couple rented Patty Duke's house in Los Angeles. The couple then moved to Cielo Drive and in March, Sharon and Roman were off to visit Rome and London. Polanski was again involved in directing and filming for United Artists. Sharon was pregnant and returned to Los Angeles on July 20, 1969, in preparation for the birth of her child.

Abigail Folger, age twenty-five,and Voytek Frykowski, age thirty-two, moved to Cielo Drive to occupy the house during the Polanskis' absence. Abigail was an heiress to the Folger Coffee fortune, graduate of Radcliffe, and for a time worked as publicity director at the University of California Art Museum in Berkeley. She later worked in a bookstore in New York City and then became involved in social work in the ghettos. It was while in New York in early 1968 that she was introduced to Voytek Frykowski. They left New York in August, driving to Los Angeles where they rented a house off Mulholland in the Hollywood Hills. Through Frykowski she met Roman Polanski and his wife, Sharon. Abigail continued in volunteer social programs that entailed long hours of attention to the ghettos of the Los Angeles area. She continued this work until the day before she and Frykowksi moved into 10050 Cielo Drive.

Voytek Frykowski and Roman Polanski had been friends in Poland; Frykowski's father reputedly had helped finance one of Polanski's early films. Voytek was regarded as a playboy, had married twice, and although he proclaimed himself a writer, no one could recall having read anything he had written. There was some controversy whether Abigail introduced Voytek to drugs so as not to lose him or whether Voytek introduced drug use to keep Abigail under his control. He had no visible means of support and apparently lived off Folger's fortune. Voytek reportedly used cocaine, LSD, mescaline, marijuana, and hashish in rather extensive quantities. An extrovert, Voytek held narcotic parties on Cielo Drive.

Jay Sebring, age thirty-five was regarded as the leading men's hair stylist in the United States. He was immaculate in appearance, drove expensive sport cars, had a butler, gave lavish parties and lived in a mansion on Easton Drive—Benedict Canyon. He was the former lover of Sharon Tate before she met Roman Polanski and remained a family friend. Sebring was a ladies' man, dating five or six different women a week, had private sexual quirks, and frequently used marijuana and cocaine.

Steve Parent, eighteen years old, lived in El Monte, a Los Angeles suburb some twenty-five miles from Cielo Drive. He had graduated from Arroya High School in June. He had a full-time job as delivery boy for a plumbing company, plus a part-time job evenings as salesman for a stereo shop. He was a studious young man and was saving his money to attend junior college that September. Steve Parent came to Cielo Drive at about 11:45 p.m. on August 8, 1969, to visit an acquaintance, William Garretson. The latter lived in the guest house to the back screened by shrubbery from the main house. The property was owned by Rudi Altobelli. He was in Europe, but had hired Garretson as a caretaker. Both youths were stereo bugs and Parent had brought a clock radio along, attempting to sell it to Garretson. The youths visited, drank a beer, and listened to stereo music. Garretson wasn't especially interested in the clock radio so Parent unplugged it at 12:25 a.m. on August 9. He put the clock radio in his white Rambler and drove off toward the electrically-controlled entrance gate that was out of sight of both houses. He never made it.

About this time in the main house, Voytek Frykowski was stretched out on a davenport asleep. Abigail Folger was in the first bedroom sitting in a chair, reading a book. Sharon Tate, heavy with child, was sitting up in bed visiting with Jay Sebring, seated on the edge of the bed. It had evidently been a quiet evening at Cielo Drive.

Four figures in the old yellow and white 1959 Ford sedan drove up the hill to the gate entrance of Cielo Drive. Charles "Tex" Watson was obvioulsy acquainted with the area, got out, climbed the telephone pole and using the wire cutters, severed the wires. They then drove back down the hill, parked the vehicle and, bringing extra clothing, walked back up. Thinking the gate might have an alarm system, the four climbed up a steep brushy incline, over a fence and were stowing their extra clothing in the bushes when they saw headlights of a car. It was coming down the driveway from inside the property toward the gate. Tex told the girls to lie down and be quiet. He went momentarily out of sight, then on the driver's side of the car, they heard his voice and another voice which said, "Please don't hurt me; I won't say anything." Then they heard a gunshot and then another gunshot, another one, and another one. Tex returned and the girls assisted him in pushing the car away from the gate, back up the driveway. In this way, for no apparent reason, Steven Parent died.

Tex and the three girls then walked up the driveway to the main house. Tex removed a screen, opened a dining room window and crawled inside, and momentarily was at the front door. Susan Atkins and Patricia Krenwinkel entered the house with Tex. Linda Kasabian stayed on the outside. The man on the davenport woke up and Tex jumped in front of him and put the .22-caliber revolver in his face and said, "Be quiet or you're dead." Frykowski replied, "Who are you, what do you want?" In court testimony, the girls related that Tex had said, "I'm the devil, and I'm here to do the devil's business." Sadie obtained a towel from the bathroom and tied Frykowski's hands behind his back. Tex then pushed him down on the davenport with hands pinned underneath.

In haste, Tex told Sadie to check for other people in the house. In the extreme southeast bedroom of the massive home was a woman reading a book; the woman smiled, and Sadie smiled back. Sadie crossed the hallway, walking west and glanced into a bedroom; a woman on the bed was talking to a man seated at the foot of the bed. Neither saw her.

Sadie returned to the living room and told Tex that there were people in the bedrooms. He told her to go and bring them out. Sadie, with knife in hand, ushered Abigail Folger out into the living room. She did the same thing on the other side of the hall, waving her knife at Jay and Sharon as they walked out into the living room. None offered resistance; they were in complete shock.

They commented, "What's going on here?" Tex, with gun in hand, ordered them to lie down on their stomachs near the fireplace. Jay Sebring pleaded for Sharon's life because of her pregnant state and in desperation lunged for the gun. Tex shot him in the armpit. Jay fell forward in front of the fireplace where Tex kicked him on the bridge of the nose. Tex ordered the others to be quiet, and he asked for their money. Abigail gave seventy-two dollars from her purse, and even offered her credit cards, which were refused. Sebring, who was lying on the floor, had a rope tied around his neck. The loose rope was thrown up over the white ceiling beam and then tied around the necks of Sharon and Abigail. Tex pulled on one side of the rope so that Sharon and Abigail had to stand up to prevent choking. Tex told Sadie to take her knife and kill Frykowski. In the ensuing struggle, he got his hand loose and grabbed Sadie by her long, flowing dark hair. In the struggle both were screaming for help, and Sadie was stabbing with her knife the best she could, several times at the man's legs. Frykowski momentarily broke free and bolted toward the door hollering for help. Tex was immediately upon him, shooting and beating him over the head with the revolver butt. Then, with his knife, Tex stabbed the best he could, while Frykowski still fought for his life.

Abigail Folger had gotten loose and was in a fight with Patricia (Katie) Krenwinkel. Tex momentarily returned to help Katie and just an instant before he stabbed Abigail once in the middle of her body—she looked up at him, relaxed and said, "I give up, take me." Tex went over to Sebring, bent down and stabbed him viciously many times in the back. Tex then told Sadie to take care of Sharon. Sadie locked her arm around Sharon's neck, forcing her onto the davenport, saying, "Woman, I have no mercy for you." Sharon is reported to have said, "Please, let me go; all I want to do is have my baby."

There was much confusion. Tex ran outside to further attend to Frykowski. He returned and ordered Susan to kill Sharon. There is some conflict in who did what but somehow Sharon was stabbed sixteen times. Abigail Folger, although mortally wounded, managed to get outside, and Katie stabbed her as she fell onto the lawn. Tex went over and stabbed her a number of times, then he went to Frykowski who was lying on the lawn to the right of the front door and kicked him in the head; the body didn't move. Sadie and "Katie" Krenwinkel were at this time trying to locate Linda Kasabian. Unknown to them, Linda was frightened from the scene and was hiding in the bushes down where they had parked the '59 Ford.

They had been instructed to leave a sign; Sadie dipped a towel in

Sharon's blood and wrote the word "pig" on the outside of the front door, which was then left open. Tex, Sadie, and Katie left and picked up the extra clothing they had hidden in the bushes. They walked down the hill to the parked '59 Ford where Linda was behind the wheel with the motor running. Tex lectured her and told her to move over so he could drive. They changed clothing in the car, all except Linda, who had not been in the house, and had no blood on her. They drove along an embankment and tossed the bundle of bloody clothes. The knives and gun were tossed out at three or four different places. Later they stopped on a side street and, using a garden hose, washed off the blood. When they pulled up at the old Spahn Movie Ranch, Charles Manson was waiting. It was about 2 a.m.

Investigating officers later learned that William Garretson had stayed up late listening to his stereo turned way up. The dogs he cared for did become disturbed and barked on two occasions during the night. Possibly he didn't hear the shots or screams or possibly he did and hid out.

Linda Kasabian later told officers she observed Frykowski emerge from the front door covered with blood and collapsed on the lawn. Later, she saw Abigail Folger running out the door with Katie stabbing her. At that moment she decided Charles Manson really wasn't Jesus Christ.

That night, Charlie didn't return to Stephanie Schram's trailer until dawn. Where did Charlie, Clem and Bruce Davis go that night? Had they checked out Cielo Drive after Tex and the girls returned to Spahn Ranch? After all, Tex reported that it was perfect, very fast with a lot of blood, and a lot of panic. To Charlie, Helter Skelter had begun. They must have been curious.

In any such tragic event, there is an immediate turmoil of activity, including a deluge of investigative procedures, inquiries from the press, radio and TV media, and necessity to notify friends and relatives. This difficult task fell to William Tennant, good friend and business manager of Roman Polanski. Through contacts with Sharon's mother, he was notified and came to Cielo Drive, identifying all victims except the youth in the white Rambler. On reaching home, William Tennant made what was, for him, the most difficult contact. He put in a call to Roman Polanski's town house in London, reporting that there had been a disaster at his Cielo Drive house. Polanski first assumed there had been a landslide or fire. Tennant hurriedly replied, "Sharon is dead, also Voytek, Abigail, and Sebring." Polanski was shocked and confused; he had talked by telephone with Sharon the day before at 11 a.m. Pacific time. That evening Roman Polanski returned from London and reporters at the Los Angeles Airport described him as a "terribly crushed" man, "beaten by the tragedy." He was taken to an apartment inside the Paramount lot, where he remained in seclusion under a doctor's care. The police talked to him briefly that night but he was unable to suggest anyone with a possible motive for the murders.

People in Los Angeles were terrified, especially Hollywood personalities. The killer or killers could be anyone. A cloud of fright hung over southern California more dense than its smog. People bought guns, and purchased guard dogs and security protection. No one knew who the police would question next. A film figure is alleged to have said, "Toilets are flushing all over Beverly Hills; the entire Los Angeles sewer system is stoned."

Roman Polanski and friends of the Polanski family offered to pay $25,000 reward to the person or persons who could furnish information leading to the arrest and conviction of the murderers of Sharon Tate, her unborn child, and the other four victims. In announcing the reward, Peter Sellers, who had put up a portion of the money, together with Warren Beatty, Yul Brynner, and others, stated: "Someone must have knowledge or suspicions they are withholding or afraid to reveal. Someone must have seen the blood-soaked clothing, the knife, the gun, the getaway car. Somebody must be able to help."

At mid-day Saturday, August 9, 1969, everything appeared quite normal at the old Spahn Movie Ranch. A few of the "Family" members were up and about. In the late afternoon, Susan "Sadie" Atkins, Charles "Tex" Watson, Patricia "Katie" Krenwinkel and Steve "Clem" Grogan watched the early evening TV news. At this time they first learned the identification of the victims at Cielo Drive. They reportedly joked and laughed about it; "The Soul sure did pick a lulu," one had said.

That evening Charlie told Sadie and others to get extra dark clothing. "We're going to go out and do the same thing we did last night, only to different houses." It was the same car, the same group—Sadie, Katie, Linda and Tex but, for some reason, Charlie, Clem and Leslie Van Houten went also.

They first stopped in front of a house in Pasadena. Charlie got out. The others drove around the block, then came back and picked him up. He had seen pictures of children through the window and did not want to "do" that house.

They stopped in front of another house, but observed some people sitting in a car nearby and after a few minutes they decided to drive on. With Linda driving, Charlie directed her to drive back to the Pasadena Freeway. After riding around Pasadena for some time, Manson took over the driving. Later he spotted a church, stopped, and said he was going to "get" the minister. Charlie came back a little later saying the church door was locked.

With Linda driving again, they spotted a white sports car. Charlie told her to "pull up alongside at the next light, I'm going to kill the driver." Linda pulled up next to the car, but just as Charlie jumped out, the light changed and the sports car sped away. Unknowingly, a most fortunate potential victim escaped.

Thus far, their wandering seemed to have no real plans nor did Charlie seem to have specific victims in mind, but immediately after the sports car incident, Charlie directed Linda to the Los Feliz section of Los Angeles near Griffith Park. He soon told her to stop at a specific house, which Linda and the others recognized.

Family members including Linda had visited the house at 3267 Waverly Drive where Harold True had lived in early 1968. True was a friend of Charlie's jail buddy Kaufman and Family members had been there for peyote and LSD parties. True had moved out in August 1968. Everyone in the car exclaimed, "You're not going to do that house, are you?" Manson replied, "No, the one next door."

About 9 p.m. on Saturday, August 9, 1969, Leno and Rosemary LaBianca and Susan Struthers, Rosemary's twenty-one-year-old daughter by a previous marriage, left Lake Isabella where they had been visiting, for the long drive back to Los Angeles. The lake, in the Kern River area, is a popular resort about 150 miles north of Los Angeles. They were driving their 1968 green Thunderbird, towing a speed boat on a trailer behind.

Leno was the president of a chain of Los Angeles supermarkets, Italian, and forty-four years of age. Rosemary, a trim, attractive brunette of thirty-eight, owned a dress shop, the Boutique Carriage, in Los Angeles, a successful enterprise. She and Leno had been married since 1959.

Because of the boat they fell behind the Saturday night traffic speedily heading toward Los Angeles. Like many others that night, they had heard the radio news of the Tate murders. Susan later reported, "Rosemary particularly appeared disturbed." It seems someone had been entering their house while they were away. "Things had been disturbed and the dogs were outside the house when they should have been inside."

About 1 a.m. on August 10, the LaBiancas dropped Susan off at her apartment on Greenwood Place, in the Los Feliz district of Los Angeles. Leno and Rosemary lived in the neighborhood at 3301 Waverly Drive.

The LaBiancas stopped at a news stand to pick up a Sunday edition of the *Herald Examiner*. Arriving home they parked the Thunderbird and boat in the driveway, removing only minor items. For unknown reasons the car and boat were not garaged and stored for the night, a normal procedure for Leno.

By this time Manson and his Family were in front of 3301 Waverly Drive. Telling the others to stay in the car, Manson got out. With leather thongs around his neck, he walked up the curving driveway toward LaBianca's house and disappeared from sight. Linda thought it was about 2 a.m. and that Charlie had stuck something in his pocket before leaving, probably a gun.

Manson suddenly returned and told Tex, Katie and Leslie to get out of the car and bring their bundles of extra clothing. Manson told the trio that there were two people in the house. He had tied them up and told them everything was going to be all right, and that they shouldn't be afraid. The LaBiancas had been set up for slaughter. Charlie didn't want all the panic of the previous night. "Don't let them know you're going to kill them," he warned. He must have told them to leave a sign. When they were finished, they were instructed to hitch-hike back to the Spahn Ranch.

What actually happened inside the LaBianca house that night can only be reconstructed from what Family members present later told Susan Atkins and Linda Kasabian as revealed in their testimony. Exact details of the tragedy were ascertained by Los Angeles Police Department investigating officers assigned to the LaBianca homicides.

Leno LaBianca looked up from his newspaper and observed a short male Caucasian, hippie-type with long hair dressed in dark clothing. Charlie told him, "Everything is going to be OK; sit down and be quiet." He located Rosemary in the bedroom and brought her into the living room. Using leather thongs he then tied Leno's and Rosemary's hands behind their backs, and then tied them together, back to back. He again assured them that they weren't going to be hurt and sat them down on the divan. Charlie then walked over to the cabinet where Rosemary had left her purse. He removed her wallet from the purse and walked out the front door, leaving it unlocked. Later, investigating officers found that the back door could easily be jimmied with a credit card, and that could have been how Charlie entered.

Family members in the '59 Ford were talking quietly when suddenly Charlie approached and looked in. He called Tex, Katie and Leslie out of the car and gave them a few final instructions. The two walked in the front door bearing their extra clothing. Entering the living room, they observed the terrified couple. A brief search of the house was made, and to avoid detection, the shades were pulled down. From a kitchen drawer they removed a wood-handled knife from a carving set, and an ivory-handled carving fork.

Katie and Leslie untied Mrs. LaBianca, took her into the bedroom, and pushed her down on the bed. She was wearing a short pink nightgown, over it a blue dress with horizontal stripes. Before the struggle ended, she had received forty-one stab wounds, thirty-six of which were to her back and buttocks. Her hands were not tied and she received a defensive wound to her left jaw. An electrical cord from one of a pair of bedroom lights was tied around her neck. In her final struggle she ended up face down on the bedroom floor and, evidently in trying to crawl, had overturned both of the bedroom lights. After she was dead, a pillowcase was slipped over her head.

Tex evidently pushed Leno onto the divan, ripping open his pajama top. He started stabbing in the front, and Leno, with his hands tied behind him, was defenseless. After the futile struggle ended, there were twelve stab wounds, plus fourteen puncture wounds made by a double-tined fork. The electric cord around his neck was attached to a massive lamp, the cord knotted so tightly it appeared to have choked him. After he was dead, a pillowcase was also slipped over his head.

Later Katie revealed that Leslie was at first hesitant to stab. And the sixteen wounds she inflicted were not necessary. Autopsy reports indicated later that the woman was already dead from Leslie's stabbings.

Katie, not to be outdone, took the double-tined fork and stabbed Leno in the abdomen. In addition to the number of stab wounds in the abdomen, someone had carved the letters WAR in his flesh.

The trio proceeded to leave bewildering signs, written in blood, at three locations in the residence. High up on the north wall in the living room above several paintings were the words DEATH TO PIGS. On the south wall, to the left of the front door, even higher up, was the single word RISE. There were two words on the refrigerator door in the kitchen, the first of which was misspelled. They read HEALTER SKELTER.

The three wiped down locations where they might have left fingerprints and went to the rear bathroom where they took showers and changed clothing. Hungry, they located food in the refrigerator. After having satisfied their hunger, leaving watermelon rinds in the kitchen sink, they left by the front door, clutching their bloody clothing. They walked a few blocks, discarded the clothing in a garbage container, and hitchhiked back to the Spahn Ranch.

Frank Struthers, Jr., Rosemary LaBianca's fifteen-year-old son, had stayed over at Lake Isabella with a friend, Jim Saffie. His family had a cabin there and the youths returned to Los Angeles in the evening of Sunday, August 10. Saffie dropped Struthers off about 8:30 p.m. at the end of the long driveway leading up to the LaBianca residence. Carrying his camping equipment up the driveway, Struthers noticed that the speedboat was still on the trailer behind Leno's Thunderbird. This seemed unusual. His stepfather never left the boat out overnight. He stowed his equipment in the garage and walked up to the back door of the residence. Momentarily he noticed the window shades were pulled down. The light was on in the kitchen. He was frightened as he knocked on the door and called out; there was no response.

Gravely concerned, he walked to a hamburger stand where there was a pay phone and called the house; there was no answer. He then called his sister and told her something was wrong at the house. Susan and her boyfriend, Joe Dorgan, arrived about 9:30 p.m., picked up Frank and drove to 3301 Waverly Drive.

Rosemary often left a set of house keys in her car that was parked in the garage. They found them and opened the back door to the residence. Dorgan suggested Susan remain in the kitchen while he and Frank checked the house. They saw Leno in the living room; he was sprawled on his back between the divan and a chair. His stomach was bare and a fork was protruding from it. They knew he was dead.

Afraid Susan would follow and worried that they might disturb evidence, Dorgan attempted to protect Susan by saying that everything was OK. They hurried down the driveway and from Dr. and Mrs. Merry J. Brigham's apartment, they called the police. Two officers arrived five to seven minutes later. After one look in the house, the officers called for backup, a supervisor, and an ambulance. Only after the ambulance arrived and nearly departed with Leno's body did they find Rosemary's body in the bedroom.

In the weeks ahead the LaBianca detectives would do a remarkable job of tracking their way through the tangled maze of Leno LaBianca's complex financial affairs. They were amazed to learn that he owned nine thoroughbred race horses and was a chronic gambler, visited the race tracks nearly every race day, betting high stakes. He was $230,000 in debt. A friend told officers he thought the murders might have been the work of the Mafia. Leno had been on the board of directors of a Hollywood bank. As a result of the investigations, several of the board members were indicted and convicted of a kiting scheme. The possibility of a Mafia link became an important lead that the investigators had to check out. Leno had no known enemies and did not have a criminal record. He died in the home where he was born, having purchased it from his mother in November of 1968.

Rosemary is believed to have been born in Mexico of American parents, and then orphaned or abandoned in Arizona. In an orphanage until the age of twelve, she was adopted by a family named Harmon, who took her to California. She met her first husband while working as a carhop in Los Feliz in the late 1940s, while still in her teens. They were divorced in 1958, and while working as a waitress at the Los Feliz Inn, she met and married Leno LaBianca.

Rosemary was reported to have a good head for business. She invested in stocks and commodities and was successful. How successful she had been was not known until her estate was probated, and it was learned that she left $2,600,000.

LaBianca detectives made a detailed search of the one-story residence. There was no evidence of robbery as a motive and among items they would log were a man's gold ring with one- carat diamond, other precious stones and diamonds, two expensive woman's rings on a dresser, necklaces, bracelets, watches, camera equipment, assorted expensive firearms, and coin collections, undisturbed. Where fingerprints should have been, there were none.

Deputy Medical Examiner David Katsuyama conducted the LaBianca autopsies. Before starting, he removed the pillowcases from the heads of the victims. Only then it was discovered that in addition to the carving fork embedded in Leno's abdomen, a knife had been thrust into his throat. The knife with a five-inch blade, had been taken from LaBianca's kitchen drawer. Other deeper wounds were made by a longer double-edged instrument, possibly a bayonet.

There were many puzzling considerations in the Tate-LaBianca murders, but at this time at least a partial pattern was discernible: the proximity of locations, consecutive nights, multiple murders, the victims' affluence, Caucasians, multiple stab wounds, no evidence of robbery, and absence of conventional motive. Yet, within twenty-four hours, the Los Angeles Police Department decided there was no connection between the two sets of murders.

·8·
Back to the Desert

On August 12, David Hannum, a blond, twenty-one-year-old man from Venice, California, arrived at Spahn Movie Ranch. Ruby Pearl, who kept books and managed the horse rentals hired him as a ranch hand. He was well- acquainted with the California deserts and Charlie started pumping him for information. Being a newcomer to Spahn, Hannum was not aware of the dimensions of the Family; Charlie kept many of the girls hidden in various hillside camps.

Hannum talked to several Family members about a twenty-six-acre ranch owned by his mother in Owens Valley near the town of Olancha west of Death Valley, somewhat secluded and consisting of a weather-beaten house, another deteriorated small residence, and some out-buildings. Everyone was unsettled at the Spahn Ranch, and Charlie was anxious to move dune buggies and supplies into the desert.

On August 14, Tex, Juan Flynn, Hannum and others loaded ranch owner George Spahn's semi-trailer with supplies, dune buggy parts, and camping equipment. With another vehicle, thought to be a milk truck and towing a dune buggy, both outfits headed for Olancha. They unloaded all the gear and drove back to the Spahn Ranch late that night. Tex and one of the girls remained behind at the Hannum Ranch. On returning to the Spahn Ranch, the Family immediately loaded the semi-trailer with more supplies. Bruce Davis, accompanied by Diane Bluestein, returned to Olancha.

Sometime late in the day August 15, Kitty Lutesinger called the Spahn Ranch and asked for someone to pick her up at her folks' horse ranch at Northridge. The seventeen-year-old pregnant by Beausoleil, was having trouble with her folks regarding the situation. She was still not aware that Beausoleil had been arrested. That evening, Sadie Glutz and another girl drove there and brought Kitty back to the Spahn Ranch.

Earlier, Charlie had encouraged members of motorcycle clubs to hang out with the Family. Two gangs closest to the Family were the Satan Slaves and the Straight Satans. He wanted the bikers to join his group to provide a needed military wing. A short, black-haired, mustached Straight Satan named Danny DeCarlo had the longest and strongest relationship of any of the bikers with the Family. He originally came by to fix a bike and decided to stay with a proffering of an endless supply of girls, who, because of his endowments, soon dubbed him Donkey Dan. DeCarlo worshipped guns and set up a munitions and gun room at the old Spahn Movie Ranch. It became a repository for knives, bayonets, rifles and shotguns.

There had been considerable friction and discontent exhibited recently between the Straight Satans and the Family. The Family's sexual behavior, unkempt appearance, and Charlie's fatalistic preaching had turned the gang off.

On Friday night, the Straight Satans came in cars and on bikes to get Danny back. They threatened to kill several male members of the Family and to burn the ranch. DeCarlo talked them out of their violent intentions. They gave him until 5 o'clock the next afternoon "to get his ass back to Venice." Some of the Family members were armed and there was a real possibility of a fight. The potentially violent confrontation was subdued to some extent by the advances of the covey of girls. The bikers eventually left, but obviously they were not to be part of Charlie's military guard.

For quite some time prior to August 16, Sgt. Bill Gleason of the Los Angeles sheriff's office at Malibu Station had been observing the Spahn Ranch with considerable interest. He had been gathering data on the Family's death threats, the alleged shooting of a Black Panther and their assembly of a number of dune buggies. He had heard from Whitely and Guenther about Kitty Lutesinger and that the Family had a sizeable firearms arsenal. Plans were made to raid the Spahn Ranch and on August 12, Gleason and detective personnel met with Deputy District Attorney Robert Schirn to review the purposes of the raid. Schirn issued a search warrant dated August 13, 1969, and Malibu Justice Court Justice John Merrick signed the warrant, valid only for the date specified.

For some unexplained reason, the officers delayed their mission until August 16. A contingent of Special Enforcement Bureau officers circled Spahn ranch just before dawn. Perhaps seventy-five or more officers were involved, some on foot and others in motor vehicles. They kicked in the doors of old movie sets and trailers and searched outlying campsites.

They hauled people out of buildings and brought others from outlying areas and placed them in a circle in front of the old movie set. Two or three girls sought to escape by running toward the creek, but they were arrested and brought back. Three children, including Tanya Kasabian, were found asleep with two of the girls and were later turned over to juvenile authorities.

Officers described the area as filthy with refuse, dune buggy parts, and related equipment strewn about. The raid netted a huge cache of firearms, including the traditional submachine gun in a violin case. An assortment of automobiles, pickup trucks, motorcycles, and four dune buggies were seized by the officers. Twenty-six people were arrested.

Most of those taken into custody were booked under pseudonyms for auto theft; the others for different offenses. They were taken first to the Malibu substation and later to the county jail in downtown Los Angeles. Within seventy-two hours, all were released; the evidence was considered insufficient and invalid because the raid had been conducted on a date other than that specified on the warrant.

Donald Jerome (Shorty) Shea and John Swartz were ranch hands at Spahn Ranch and had explored ways of ridding the ranch of the Family. Manson got word of this and threatened Swartz, "I could kill you at any time. I can come into your quarters any time." Swartz, in fear, left the ranch shortly after.

Shorty Shea, thirty-six, had worked on the Spahn Ranch off and on for some fifteen years as a horse wrangler. He frequently had bit parts in western movies. When the prospect of an acting job materialized, he would quit work and go in search of that ever-elusive stardom. He had been conferring with George Spahn and wanted to be put in charge so he could throw Charlie and his Family off the ranch. Shorty had also heard a few things about the Tate-LaBianca murders and was suspicious.

Charlie, Clem and Bruce reportedly returned to the ranch on August 26 or 27, and tortured Shorty, taking turns sticking him with knives and bayonets. Nearly the entire Family was involved in the pro-longed death process. Shorty kept hollering and screaming and just wouldn't die. They ended up beheading him and cutting him in nine pieces. The remains were put in a depression and covered with leaves. Later the girls would re-bury the body parts near the railroad tracks.

In late August, Bill Vance and Vern Plumlee went to Portland, Oregon, and brought back two youths, Diane Von Ahn and Ed Bailey, to add to the Family. They hung around the Spahn Ranch for a few days, conducting a number of burglaries before joining Manson and the Family in Death Valley.

In early September, the Family started moving to the desert In various rented and stolen vehicles. They shuttled back and forth from the Los Angeles area, bringing supplies and people to their desert paradise. The Hannum Ranch provided a base for moving into outlying remote sections of the desert. A few members went directly to the Barker-Myers area in Goler Wash. By mid-September of 1969, Hannum Ranch had been vacated and most of the Family roamed in and out of Goler Wash.

About September 1, Bruce Davis, Tex Watson and Brenda McCann, also known as Nancy Laura Pittnam, drove a dune buggy up Goler Wash to the Barker Ranch, Where they met miner Paul Crockett, Brooks Poston, and Paul Watkins. All had previously heard from Watkins about the remarkable Crockett. Bruce reportedly delivered Charlie's message, "He's down below at Sourdough Springs; if he has your permission, he'll come up." Bruce Davis drove the dune buggy down the wash to relay Crockett's message. A little while later Charlie drove into the yard behind Bruce in another dune buggie with a contingent of girls.

Everybody gathered inside the main house and there was a confrontation between Charlie and Crockett. Charlie bragged about all the gear he was moving into the desert and the imminent doom he called Helter Skelter. Crockett wasn't visibly impressed. In frustration Charlie walked over to where Brooks Poston was seated and threatened to cut his throat by pulling his head back and laying a knife against his throat. Brooks kept his head, and Charlie returned to baiting Crockett. It was a stand-off. With tension in the air, Charlie and his Family left and headed for Myers Ranch, about one-half mile east, where they planned to stay.

Crockett, Poston, and Watkins talked late into the night about whether to leave Barker Ranch that night or stay. Crockett didn't buy Charlie's fear tactics, and there was mining to be done. Crockett may have been intrigued by Charlie and part of his motivation for staying was prompted by his own curiosity. The trio was unaware that the Family had committed the most gruesome murders in California history only weeks before.

A few days later, additional Family members arrived at the Myers Ranch, including Brenda, Juan Flynn, Gypsy, and Clem. Juan, the tall Panamanian ranch hand, spent only two days at Myers Ranch. He knew too much, and Charlie threatened earlier to carve him up. He spent a few days over in Butte Valley and then moved down to Barker Ranch and Crockett's little island of sanity.

Meanwhile, more supplies arrived for Charlie. Food, camping gear, weapons, and stolen dune buggies came in a steady stream. Charlie continued to send contingents of women down to Barker Ranch in an effort to entice lost brethren back to the Family. When that failed, he appeared with Clem and Tex, brandishing shotguns, discharging them around the ranch. Crockett and the others shrugged off these demonstrations, and Crockett even engaged Charlie in a long verbal exchange of an unthreatening nature. Charlie's inability to frighten or frustrate Crockett left him somewhat confused.

Crockett, Flynn, Watkins, and Poston had been sleeping on cots in the bunkhouse at the Barker Ranch. They placed a loaded shotgun on the wall for protection. Juan was especially nervous about what

Charlie might do, but Crockett assured them, "He can't sneak up on us here, we'll hear him and wake up."

One night, after midnight, they all woke up and Juan grabbed the shotgun and walked outside. Charlie, Clem and Bruce were caught sneaking around. Juan called to them by name, in the darkness, not knowing who was there. Charlie came in. Obviously he had lost his nerve and exhibited frustration. With a grin, he threatened that he would succeed some time. Crockett told him, "There ain't no such thing as sneaking up on people." Charlie turned and walked out the door.

A couple of nights later they all woke up simultaneously. Crockett remarked, "He doesn't give up, does he?" sitting there in silence, they observed Charlie push the door open and crawl inside on his hands and knees.

They immediately spoke to him.

"Lose something, Charlie?"

"One of these nights," he replied in obvious frustration, and he arose and went out of the door. They heard him say something to Tex and Bruce as the three of them left.

Crockett suggested, "Let's go down to the main house and have a little pow wow."

Crockett sensed the frustration of Charlie and the inherent dangers, but he wasn't about to let someone drive him away from the canyon. He had been content to observe and tolerate Charlie, but now things felt a bit out of hand.

His prospecting had just begun to be successful.

"We'll stay one more week," Crockett told his companions. Watkins and Flynn left the next morning for Las Vegas to obtain supplies. Juan was fearful at the turn of events at the Barker Ranch and decided to hitchhike to Los Angeles and collect money that George Spahn owed him. From there, he wasn't sure where he would go.

Crockett and Poston were now alone at Barker Ranch. They realized how vulnerable they were to Charlie's threats and decided to leave. The next night they packed up a few provisions and hiked eighteen miles in the dark to the talc mines where they hitched a ride to Shoshone.

Watkins returned to Barker Ranch a few days later and much to his surprise found the Family had taken over the whole of the ranch. Charlie attempted to convince Watkins that his place was in the Family. Watkins was very worried about Crockett and Poston, and Charlie implied that they "were no more." Shortly after that, Watkins left. Later, to his surprise, he found both Poston and Crockett alive and well in Shoshone.

◄9►
Suspicions & Maneuvers at Goler Wash

On August 18, 1969, Deputy Sheriff Dennis Cox of Lone Pine observed a young girl spaced out and wandering around at Olancha in Owens Valley. She appeared to be on speed or acid; he took her to the sheriff's office in Independence. She gave her name as Diane Bluestein, age sixteen, and other limited information. Checks on the girl came back negative so Cox drove her back to Olancha in an attempt to find people with whom she might be traveling or living. He finally located some hippies at the Hannum Ranch where she had been staying.

There were two men and one girl at the place. One of the men gave his name as "Charley Montgomery" and the girl was addressed as "Gypsy." A semi-trailer flatbed truck, a dune buggy, food, camping supplies, and auto parts were in the back yard. The people were vague and uncommunicative, so Cox decided to keep them under surveillance and left Diane in their care. Later Cox was to learn that the second man was Bruce Davis and that Montgomery was really Charles Denton Watson. Gypsy was Katherine Share.

Cox had observed that the Hannum Ranch group was absent from the area frequently, often on nocturnal forays into the desert and surrounding towns. People in the small town of Olancha were vocal in their complaints about this particular band of hippies, their scrounging, panhandling, and brazen behavior in the presence of local citizenry. Cox began writing field investigation report cards. On August 21 he noted, "Charles Montgomery, 23, DOB 12/2/45, male, caucasian, 6 ft. slim build, ruddy complexion. Notation—Loitering."

Game Warden Vern Burandt of Lone Pine also received complaints from several residents about hippies killing quail, defecating where they pleased, and swimming nude in the creek. When a citizen, a man named Duvalt, called to complain, Burandt drove out to see him.

When Burandt asked Duvalt to accompany him across a field to the Hannum Ranch, Duvalt was hesitant. "They are sure as hell a cruddy, motley outfit," he said. The men finally went over and found no one there. Burandt found evidence that game birds had been killed but was more amazed at the mess around the place. As Cox had reported, they found auto parts, camping equipment, and tools. Burandt found a fully-loaded Winchester 97 shotgun in a shed. He thought he would keep an eye on the place and planned a later return.

Meanwhile, Cox was observing more dune buggies and hippies coming and going from the Hannum Ranch. He made the long trip into the Saline Valley over rough mining roads in an attempt to learn the group's interest in that area. In the maze of primitive roads, their tracks were all over the place, but he was unable to ascertain where in the desert they were caching food and other supplies.

Another time, some of the group members pulled out of the Hannum Ranch during the night. Cox had information they probably headed for Panamint Valley. He checked out the vehicles observed earlier at Hannum Ranch. The flatbed semi-trailer was registered to George Spahn of Chatsworth and the dune buggy to a male resident of Santa Susana Pass Road, Chatsworth. Neither vehicle was reported stolen.

In early September, there was a flurry of activity at Hannum Ranch, involving several dune buggies and a number of hippies. By the time the deputies were ready to give the ranch a thorough searching, the hippies had vanished and the Hannum Ranch had been cleaned out.

On September 29, 1969, California Highway Patrol Officer James Pursell of the Death Valley post and Ranger Dick Powell traveled into the Goler Wash area from the east side of the Panamint Mountains by way of Butte Valley to check out two dwellings in the area. At Barker Ranch they found two women about eighteen or nineteen years old. The two were uncommunicative and said the man who lived there had gone to Ballarat, and that he would be back later. Pursell and Powell started down the canyon and met an early-model orange Dodge Powerwagon truck, driven by Paul Crockett, the person for whom they were looking. He was accompanied by a young man who gave his name as Brooks Poston.

Crockett expressed surprise when he was told there were two women at the Barker Ranch, where Crockett had been staying. "They were not there when I left," he said. In his truck Crockett had three cases of motor oil, new automobile batteries, new tire tubes, auto tune-up parts and a commercial movie camera. He said the load had been brought up from Panamint Valley by a hippie group, hand-carried across a dry rock falls, and reloaded on the truck to be taken to the Barker ranch. When Crockett was asked why he would volunteer the use of his truck, he indicated his life might depend on doing what was asked of him.

The battery was low on Crockett's Power wagon, and he couldn't restart it. Pursell and Powell decided that Crockett and Poston should return to the Barker Ranch for a detailed interrogation. When they arrived, the two young women were gone, but the officers felt that they were observing from some nearby point.

Unbelievable and fantastic information was given the two officers by Crockett and Poston. They told tales of drug use, sex orgies, the actual attempt to recreate the days of Rommel and the Desert Corps by tearing over the desert at night in dune buggies, and the stringing of field telephone lines around the area for rapid communication. Crockett and Poston also reported that the leader of the group believed he was Jesus Christ. He had created a cult of some sort. Poston reported that he had been connected with the group at one time but had since broken ties with them.

The men discussed the abortive raid on the Spahn Ranch, the resulting recovery of stolen dune buggies, and the ultimate release of those arrested for lack of evidence. Crockett and Poston were sure the group was camped nearby, and when the officers left, the two miners were sure they could expect a visit from the Family to learn what had been discussed.

In the yard was a rail-type dune buggy from which Pursell obtained the vehicle identification for a later check. The buggy was without an engine at the time.

The officers left Barker Ranch and drove west toward Sourdough Spring, where they detected vehicle tracks going into a side wash. They drove up the wash a short distance and parked their Jeep. Now on foot, the officers separated, Powell hiking up one ridge, and Pursell up the opposite ridge.

About a quarter of a mile up the wash, Powell spotted some nude or semi-nude women in the brush and motioned Pursell to join him. Powell told the women to get dressed, and they led the officers on up the wash, where they encountered several other scantily-clad females, until there was a total of seven, all about eighteen to twenty years of age. Near this location was a red 4x4 Toyota and two hippie men. The two men started to move away and were told by the officers to stop, they needed to talk to them. One, small in stature, ran from the area and Powell gave chase but lost him in the rough terrain. Concerned for the safety of Pursell, Powell returned to the Jeep and drove it up the wash near the hippie camp. The other man gave his name to Pursell as Charlie Montgomery. He said he had been hitch-hiking on Highway 395 near Olancha, was picked up by the group and had just arrived in the area. Pursell noticed two firearms in scabbards on the vehicles and recorded their serial numbers. Both were 12-gauge shotguns.

In the camp were sleeping bags, clothing and canvas tarps, which partially concealed the vehicles. Pursell recorded the identification numbers on the two vehicles. The Toyota did not have a license plate. Pursell and Powell interviewed the hippies briefly, but they gave absolutely no reasonable information on their purpose in being in the desert.

At this time Powell noticed that the smallish man he had chased had returned and was hiding in some brush behind the Jeep. He had what appeared to be a rifle and apparently was prepared to use it if the officers attempted to take anyone into custody.

Radio communication was impossible in this isolated area and lacking any positive information, Pursell and Powell returned to their Jeep. The man previously hiding there was not observed. They then drove down treacherous Goler Wash to Panamint Valley to a location north of Ballarat, where they were successful in making radio contact with Park Service headquarters. They asked for a check on the identification of the three vehicles. Chief Ranger Leach called back later that two of the vehicles had been reported stolen. Pursell asked Leach to contact California Highway Patrol Sgt. Ray Hailey at Lone Pine for support and instructions.

After a plan of action was formulated for re-entry into the Barker Ranch, Pursell and Powell decided to go back to Ballarat for a cold drink. The folks at the combination store and restaurant insisted that the officers have dinner there. They were interested in the men's work and worried about the time their efforts might take.

Dinner was leftover fried hamburger, very well done, and overly-fried beans. They didn't eat much and after dinner headed for the mouth of Goler Wash to secure the place and spend the night.

The men sat in the darkness of Panamint Valley in that little Jeep with only the two seats in front, and no sleeping bags or blankets. They finally decided to try to get a little shut-eye, but neither of them had any desire to flop on the ground.

Finally, Pursell decided to get up on the fiberglass top, while Powell stretched out across the front seat, half of him hanging out one side. Pursell did fairly well on the roof, but every time he moved, the top would pop and snap as if it were about to collapse. They got very little sleep.

Sgt. Hailey received Leach's message relating the circumstances and Pursell and Powell's position at Goler Wash about 8 p.m. September 29. Pursell wanted Deputy Don Ward of Shoshone to set up a check point on the east side of Death Valley at Butte Valley just west of Warm Spring Mining Camp as soon as possible. Hailey advised Lt. Hurlbut at Bishop of the situation. After contact by the California Highway Patrol, Inyo County Undersheriff D. C. Lindergren dispatched Ward immediately to the Butte Valley area. From Lone Pine, Deputies Cox and J. Hildreth were told to meet Officers Parker and Doug Manning at Panamint Springs Resort at 2 a.m. September 30.

That morning, these four officers met Pursell and Powell fourteen miles south of Ballarat at the mouth of Goler Wash. In Parker's personal Toyota 4-wheel-drive, all six proceeded up the wash at 4 a.m. As they approached the rock falls, some of the riders decided to climb over the falls on foot. Parker was burning rubber despite his balloon tires. After passing the rock falls, the breathless climbers decided to ride.

For the next two miles the ascent was more gradual. Former habitations were checked out and the officers quenched their thirst at the clear springs along the way. They observed no one in the vicinity of the Lotus Mine and Sourdough Spring.

Within two miles of the Barker Ranch, Pursell and Powell decided to proceed on foot. When they arrived there, they knocked on the door and aroused a Shepherd dog inside. Crockett and Poston, who were asleep when the officers arrived, said the group they were seeking had possibly left the area. They appeared surprised to see the officers again.

The day before, just after the officers left, Charlie, the small guy that Powell had chased, had run into the house and grabbed a double-barreled shotgun off the wall. He ran out without saying a word, and later they heard two shots. Crockett told the officers that as soon as Powell and Pursell had left the day before, the suspects had also pulled a complete Volkswagen engine from under a pile of trash and installed it in the rail dune buggy, previously identified by Pursell's CHP, and had driven off within two hours.

Powell and Pursell were joined by the other members of the search party and went on to the Myers ranch. No suspects were seen in either of the areas, so they went on to Willow Spring and Anvil Spring Canyon.

That same day California Highway Patrol Officers Journigan, Anderson and Hailey left Lone Pine about 1:30 a.m. with a CHP cruiser and Hailey's 4x4 Toyota. They met Chief Ranger Leach around 4 a.m. at Park Service headquarters in Death Valley and all of them, plus Ranger Paul Fodor and Dick Powell's wife, Sheila, serving as a matron, met Don Ward and Special Deputy Tad Kanzaki in Butte Valley just north of Warm Springs. They proceeded toward the Barker Ranch, where they were to rendezvous with the other officers, but because of the severity of the terrain, they left the patrol cruiser and the sheriff's vehicle.

Existing and former habitations were checked along the route through Butte Valley.

Near Anvil Spring the party coming up from the east side was advised by miners that two vehicles loaded with people had been observed leaving the area the previous evening. The officers located the spot where tire tracks turned off the road they were on and took another faint road that led to Willow Spring in Anvil Canyon. They reached a dry creek bed and cabin a little off the road, which they searched with no results. A little later they reached two dune buggies that had been carefully concealed, the tracks wiped out with branches and more branches piled to hide the vehicles which were covered with camouflage material.

One of the dune buggies was a 1967 model, which checked out to have been stolen in Los Angeles. The second, a 1962 model, was also determined from identification numbers, to have been stolen in Los Angeles. An attempt was made to start the two vehicles, but one was out of gas and the other had a dead battery.

In such an inaccessible area, a tow truck would have been of little or no help, so the officers removed the distributor caps and the spark plug wires.

Caches of miscellaneous items were found hidden in the willows within fifty feet of the dune buggies, including tires, tubes, motor oil, fan belts, and much more, some of which Pursell identified as items he saw in Crockett's truck on September 29.

Both groups of officers now followed tire tracks in various directions. One track appeared to have been made by a 4x4 Toyota.

Obvious attempts were made by the suspects to cover their tracks—driving in circles, going over rocky terrain, and brushing out tracks when they left the circle.

A patrol plane from Bishop came to Furnace Creek with Lt. Hurlbut, and picked up Chuck Tobin with a Park Service radio. They covered the area in mid-morning, searching ravines and canyons. They reported that whoever was in the area with vehicles seemed to be playing war games; they had observed tracks in every direction. Tracks extended a long way toward Wingate Wash to the southeast and even into the Naval Weapons Test Station range.

The search of September 30 terminated in Goler Wash toward evening. As they went out the officers investigated inactive mines and old cabins but found no evidence of their hippie suspects.

An observation that would later prove embarrassing was an aircraft wing fuel tank found in Anvil Canyon. It was a type released by military aircraft, and this made the men assume that it had been jettisoned by an aircraft out of China Lake. The officers walked around the tank asking, "Where in hell do these clowns get all the gasoline to play around like this?"

Later, the officers would find another wing tank south of Barker Ranch and learn that the one they had passed this day had been half full of gasoline. The tanks were later found to have been stolen off a surplus lot in Los Angles, and were known to have been fuel storage for the Family.

Those participating in the September 30 search were disappointed. The net result of all the planning seemed to be two inoperable dune buggies and no suspects. The men wondered if the hippies had somehow learned of their plans, but it was more likely they were spooked because of the visit of Powell and Pursell the previous day. They had vacated Goler Wash.

From information Powell and Pursell garnered from Crockett and Poston, there still lingered the thought that this same group was sought in the raid on the old Spahn Movie Ranch at Chatsworth. Officers there had recovered stolen vehicles and an arsenal of firearms, including a Tommy gun in a violin case.

A feeling existed among the six patrolmen, four deputies, and three rangers, that they had only scratched the surface in this wide expanse of barren desert. As a result of the Goler Wash search, however, the Family members dispersed to various locations to minimize their detection. They came to Barker Ranch only occasionally, late in the evening, under the cover of darkness, to eat or sleep. Most departed at dawn to hide in mine tunnels or other vantage points to watch for anyone coming into the area. They packed food and water to their hideouts in case the officers returned. Later, they were to reveal that they were afraid and anxious in their endurance to Charlie's hostility. "We were confused, living by night, hiding by day, fearful, threatened by a maniac," one of the girls recalled in court testimony.

About October 1, two girls, camped out at Lotus Mine relative newcomers to the Family and fearing bodily harm at the hands of Charlie, decided to leave Goler Wash. Bo Rosenberg (Barbara Hoyt) and Simi Valley Sherri (Sherry Ann Cooper) fled from the Death Valley hideout believing, that Charlie and other members were temporarily absent. They hiked to Ballarat, where Charlie caught up with them Because other people were present, he let them go and even gave them $20 for bus fare to Los Angeles. Bo Rosenberg had been present at Spahn Ranch when Shorty Shea had been tortured and murdered by Family members. She had heard his screams that night and later the comments about how everyone took turns stabbing him and how Clem had finally cut off his head. At Barker ranch she had heard graphic accounts of other murders. Bewildered by the September 30 raid by the officers and fearing reprisal because she knew too much, she fled the area. Later she would nearly pay with her life for cooperating with law enforcement agencies.

Early in October of 1969, the Family was in constant and erratic movement in the desert. Three male members were sent to Los Angeles to bring back Barbara and Sherri, perhaps to kill them. Danny DeCarlo, part-time Family member and Straight Satan biker, foiled their efforts to secure Sherri, who was with him in Venice. New faces, male and female, showed up at the Barker Ranch. Other Family members were in Owens Valley. Bruce Davis and Clem were in Los Angeles. Clem came back with Randy Morglea. Their daylight activities were limited; there was unrest in the Death Valley hideout. Only under cover of darkness did the Family members feel somewhat secure.

Early on the night of October 2, Fillipo Tenerelli, a biker from Culver City, was found shot in a motel room at Bishop in Owens Valley. The coroner first thought it could have been suicide. Three days later, the California Highway Patrol recovered a blue 1969 Volkswagen over the cliff at Crowley Point off Highway 190 between Lone Pine and Death Valley. The vehicle had blood on the seats and floorboards. It was traced to Fillipo Tenerelli, a missing person. He had been a member of the Gypsy Jokers' biker group and was known to the Manson Family.

On the night of October 3, the man known to the officers as Charlie Montgomery, whose real name was Charles Denton Watson, took the Dodge Powerwagon and drove down Goler Wash, leaving Barker Ranch far behind. Tex, as the Family knew him, may have been fearful that the end was in sight and perhaps murder was playing on his conscience. South of Ballarat he took a shortcut toward Trona road and mired the Powerwagon down in the salt flat lake bed. He hitch-hiked out of the area and was later located at his McKinney, Texas, home. The sheriff who picked up Watson for the Los Angeles Police Department was his second cousin, Tom Montgomery.

Crockett and Poston showed up in Shoshone October 2, having hiked out over extremely difficult terrain under cover of darkness from Barker Ranch through Butte Valley to the talc mining camp near Warm Spring, a distance of eighteen miles. They had then caught a ride to Shoshone with a miner. Crockett told Deputy Sheriff Ward he felt his usefulness at Barker had ended, and he did not want to stay around waiting for the liquidation. Deputy Sheriff Ward held a taped interview with Crockett and Poston in his home on October 3, which rather mystified Ward. They told Ward of sex orgies, satanic worship, rituals, Rommel in the desert, dune buggy forays, and they implied that the Family's leader believed himself to be Jesus Christ. Ward's incredulous reaction was much like Pursell and Powell's. He wondered about the man's sanity. Poston told that Charlie had given him a knife and told him to go to Shoshone and kill the deputy sheriff, Ward. By this time, Poston was pretty well off acid and this, with Crockett's favorable influence, helped him to escape the zombie influence of the drugs. Poston also revealed that Charlie wanted Ward killed for coming to the Barker Ranch on March 16, and he had not forgotten Ward's search of Charlie in Shoshone.

Ward took the tape Crockett and Poston had made to Sheriff Merrill Curtis at Independence, nearly 200 miles over the mountains in Owens Valley. His purpose was to impress on Curtis that something evil was going on out there in the desert where law enforcement had almost never been a problem. Curtis listened to the tape, became highly agitated, yanked the tape off the machine and hurled it violently across the office. This action reflected his complete disbelief that anything so described could ever happen. He chewed Ward out for wasting his time on the matter. Ward later related brief details of the Crockett-Poston interview to Chief Ranger Leach and Superintendent Bob Murphy in Death Valley National Monument.

California Highway Patrol Officer Jim Pursell continued to check on possible auto thefts and went to Shoshone to listen to Ward's tape on Crockett and Poston. He called his superior, Sgt. Ray Hailey in Lone Pine to urge continued investigation of the auto thefts. He casually mentioned Ranger Powell's suspicion that the hippie group may have been responsible for offenses other than auto theft.

◄10►

An Investigation is Planned and Carried Out

A round-robin of discussion within the Highway Patrol brought Dave Steuber, an auto theft investigator, into the case. He established liaison with the National Auto Theft Bureau, Kern County and Los Angeles County sheriffs' departments, the Los Angeles Police Department and several credit card companies. Steuber arrived in Inyo County October 9 to assist in the investigations.

On the day of Steuber's arrival, Officer Pursell, while investigating an abandoned auto near the Talc Mining Camp at Warm Spring, learned from some four-wheelers that hippies were back in Goler Wash. This information was relayed to park headquarters at Furnace Creek. In Lone Pine, Sgt. Hailey was told of Powell's observations, but Hailey was advised that Sheriff Curtis was not eager to engage in an apprehension for auto theft. Hailey was to coordinate the raid with the assistance of Steuber, and they set out to gather manpower. Leach called the Inyo County sheriff but found him reluctant to commit deputies in a second raid he thought might not be successful. Curtis questioned the validity of the whole enterprise, and expressed the opinion that it was "a wild goose chase."

At the request of Hailey, Powell was sent late in the evening of October 9 to the mouth of Goler Wash in Panamint Valley to keep the area under surveillance and guide other officers to the Barker Ranch on October 10. Powell arrived at Goler Wash to find a blue Volkswagen parked in the area. He hid his Jeep and remained out of sight.

There had been much talk about shotguns, revolvers and maybe machine guns in the hippie arsenal. It was not unusual for the officers to become nervous in the dark of the desert. Two highway patrolmen, George and Journigan from Lone Pine, arrived at Goler Wash about 2 a.m. October 10 in a patrol cruiser. They did not observe Powell's Jeep and assumed they were the first to arrive. Eating sandwiches and talking, they did not notice Powell's silent approach until he said, "Hi."

"You damn near sent us into orbit," George declared.

Journigan told Powell, "Don't you ever do that again, or I'm liable to blow your ass away."

About 3:30 a.m. they were joined by Highway Patrolmen Anderson, Reed and Hailey, and made plans to enter Goler Wash. Meanwhile, Leach and Pursell had driven into Butte Valley early in the evening of October 9 in a Park Service carry-all and stopped at a residential mining claim where the owner was reluctant to talk, but did say he allowed the Family to store gasoline there. The officers checked out the two inoperative dune buggies stored in the area below Willow Spring.

In late evening, Ranger Schneider arrived with Highway Patrol Officer Jack O'Neil and Steuber. At midnight the officers settled down at Anvil Spring to wait.

District Attorney Frank Fowles had become interested in the case and in the absence of interest by the sheriff, decided to have members of his staff present during the raid. In the event there was an auto theft ring, he would be faced "with a hell of a lot of prosecutions." With staff members present, Fowles would be in a better position to exercise judgment in filing charges. Fowles assigned his deputy, L. H. "Buck" Gibbons, and Special Investigator Jack Gardiner to the case. They accompanied Patrol Lt. H. M. Hurlbut and the game warden, Vern Burandt, on the raid.

About 3:30 a.m. October 10, Schneider transported Steuber and Pursell to Mengel Pass. From here the officers were to hike to the Barker Ranch area. Schneider returned to Anvil Spring and hauled Leach and O'Neil to Willow Spring. They were to travel on foot across country, a little more than four miles, to the Myers Ranch. Schneider stayed at Mengel Pass where he could maintain radio contact with park headquarters at Furnace Creek and protect the vehicles parked on the pass.

Leach and O'Neil started hiking by flashlight at 4 a.m. over the sparsely vegetated desert. It was fairly easy going for them along the open wash, over the divide, and down into the side drainage of upper Goler Wash. It was still very dark when they saw the first sign of activity ahead and to their right. They saw lights flashing on some distant hills and heard the sound of a far-away vehicle. Their advance became more wary as dawn began to break.

Using a topographical map, they followed a ridge line that would take them into Barker Ranch from the northeast. The officers were near the Myers Ranch, moving quietly, when they suddenly heard voices below in the dry wash. As they came down the ridge, they could make out three figures and heard a baby cry about 200 feet away. There were people gathered around what apparently was a campsite. Cautiously, Leach and O'Neil proceeded toward the Barker Ranch. Pursell and Steuber had arrived without incident from Mengel Pass and by radio informed Leach and O'Neil of their location.

The officers were now just north of the Barker Ranch with Leach and Steuber in one location and Pursell and O'Neil nearby, awaiting the men who were coming up Goler Wash from the west.

Patrolmen Journigan, George, Anderson, Reed and Hailey, and Ranger Powell started up Goler Wash about 4 a.m. in Hailey's Toyota. They encountered the dry rock falls and some of the men got out to walk ahead and lighten the load. A little way up the canyon, Journigan and George walked right up on two male hippies sleeping in the bottom of the dry wash. Hailey almost drove his Toyota over them in the dark. Between the two on the tarp on which they were sleeping was a sawed-off 12-gauge shotgun and a bandolier of twenty-four shotgun shells loaded with deadly double O buckshot.

The two, Steven Dennis Grogan, seventeen, known in the Family as Clem Tufts, and Hugh Rocky Todd, eighteen, Family name Randy Morglea, were aroused from sleep and placed under arrest. Clem gave Journigan a little hassle but they were handcuffed and marched ahead of the Toyota. They were progressing too slowly to keep their appointed meeting with the others at Barker Ranch, so they located a heavy ore car and cuffed the two young men together through the iron spokes of a wheel.

Unknown to the officers, Clem and Randy had been stalking Stephanie Schram and Kitty Lutesinger, two seventeen-year-olds, who had fled the Barker Ranch the previous evening in fear of their lives.

As the officers prepared to leave, one of the youths demanded to know, "You gonna leave us here?" Assuring the pair they would be back, they told them that if they could carry off the ore car, they were free. The officers examined the shotgun, which was loaded, especially the operation which had altered its length. It looked "like it had been cut off with an axe."

Near Lotus Mine, one of the officers thought he saw someone peering over a rock. Journigan located him in his rifle scope and flushed out an eighteen-year-old man who gave the name of Soupspoon, true name Robert Ivan Lane. His only attire was a pair of Levis. Soupspoon was left handcuffed by one wrist to a pipeline running from Sourdough Spring to the mine and the height of the water line above ground left the victim with considerable concern as to how long he could tolerate a standing position.

Soupspoon was too far from the ranch to be acting as a lookout but was probably searching for Clem and Randy. Now that the light was

Lookout Post on ridge south of Barker Ranch. National Park Service photo

good the officers drove off, saying they would be back as soon as possible.

The officers at Barker attempted to contact the Goler Wash party by radio, but without success at first because they kept the volume down. In the absolute silence of the desert morning, the sound seemed to boom across the terrain. Finally contact was made with the Goler Wash party, and it came as a surprise that they were taking prisoners along the way. When the Goler Wash bunch arrived at Barker, they had no prisoners with them.

Leach and Steuber thought their position was quite secure, well hidden from the Barker house. As it became light, they thought they observed a lookout post, a sort of a dug-out, high on the opposite slope, which looked directly down on them. They were still trying to figure out what to do when a woman came out of the draw below them and walked toward the house. She had only to look in their direction and she would have seen one park ranger and one Highway Patrol officer trying to look like a couple of rocks. But she didn't look their way.

As dawn broke and the light increased, Pursell and O'Neil saw the same dugout on the south slope that O'Neil identified as the opening of a cave or prospect hole of some sort. A short time later three persons came out of the hole into the open, stretched, walked about briefly and returned to the dugout.

If they had looked across the ravine they could have seen the officers who were exposed on the open hillside. O'Neil decided he would take a position above the opening to cover it when the others arrived at the ranch.

To prevent detection, he walked east up a ridge behind the ranch, crossed the wash, climbed another ridge on the south side and came back down to a position above the hole. The makeshift cave had a sheet metal roof and the panoramic view made it ideal for a lookout post. When the raid started, O'Neil dropped a rock on the sheet metal roof and shouted for the people to come out with their hands up, which they did. All three were young girls. Later they asked why the officers had shot at them: The rock hitting the corrugated metal must have sounded like a shot.

The officers coming up Goler Wash had been warned by Pursell on the radio to watch out for the lookout post. Reed bailed out with his rifle and covered the lookout from behind an old tractor tire by the roadside.

Hailey drove his Toyota right up into the front yard. Powell would later remark, "Like the Sands of Iwo Jima, we ran zigzagging toward the house and bunkhouse." Journigan, followed by Steuber, hit the back door and George stood to the side of the front door. Suddenly a figure bolted out the front door. Journigan too came out the front door and tackled the fleeing figure who turned out to be Madaline Joan Cottage, Little Patty. She had a long-bladed hunting knife strapped to her side that George took to be a gun. Other officers converged on the scene, including Hurlbut with representatives of the District Attorney's Office, and Burandt.

At this time, Leach, O'Neil, and another officer were moving the three women down from the lookout post. Leach followed a ground telephone line up the slope to another lookout but found no one.

After things were under control at the Barker Ranch, several officers left for the Myers Ranch and took the three women and two babies into custody.

Leach and another officer spotted two women in a dry wash about 100 yards to the northwest. As they moved toward them, one took off running. Leach ran after her, but she was soon out of sight around a bend. He caught sight of her one more time as she turned up a side draw. She had shed some of her clothing and appeared to be nearly naked. Although he paralleled her course, he did not sight her again. Pursell called him on the radio and together they checked up the canyon to where Steuber and others had found the red Toyota. The men joked with Leach and he remarked, "A 100-yard dash in soft sand isn't my speciality. Just as well I didn't catch her as there wasn't much left to grab onto."

Barker Ranch, Manson girls awaiting transport out of Goler Wash; seated right to left Squeaky Fromme, Susan Atkins, Ruth Morehouse. Burandt photo

Arrested at the lookout post were Louella Maxwell Alexandria, twenty, true name Leslie Van Houten; Marnie Kay Reeves, twenty-one, true name Patricia Krenwinkel and Manon Minette, twenty, true name Catherine Share.

Arrested inside the Barker House were Elizabeth Elaine Williamson, twenty, true name Lynette Fromme, known to the Family as Squeaky, and Donna Kay Powell, twenty-five, true name Susan Atkins and known to the Family as Sadie Mae Glutz.

Arrested at the ranch site was Linda Baldwin, twenty-three, true name Madaline Joan Cottage.

Arrested in the canyon behind the Myers Ranch was Sandra Collins Pugh, twenty-five, maiden name Sandra Collins Good, and called Sandy.

Arrested in another canyon behind the Myers Ranch were Rachel Susan Morse, seventeen, true name Ruth Ann Morehouse, and Mary Ann Schwarm, twenty-one, true name Diane Von Ahn.

Arrested in the rocks above the Myers house was Cydette Perell, eighteen, true name Nancy Pitnam, and also known as Brenda McCann.*

In all, ten women were taken to the front yard of the Barker Ranch.

*Ages given by subjects were later found in error, many were much younger.

Sandra Collins was carrying a baby about one-year-old, who had been named Zezozose Zadfrack Glutz. He had scabs over his nose and under the left eye, having been injured in some manner several days earlier. Rachel Morse was also carrying a baby who appeared to be about two to three months old and was called Sunstone Hawk. He had a badly-sunburned face. From the actions of Pugh and Morse, the officers assumed they were their children, respectively, but later they were to find that Susan Atkins was the mother of Zezozose and Sandy Pugh the mother of Sunstone.

Hailey and Pursell decided it was time to go back down Goler Wash and bring Soupspoon, Clem and Randy back to the Barker ranch. On their return they isolated their handcuffed prisoners from the women.

Steuber and George, accompanied by Deputy District Attorney Gibbons, were guarding the women. Susan Atkins approached the officers and, pointing to Clem, asked the officers to "unhook him." When George asked the reason he was told, "I want to take him behind the buildings and make love to him one more time." She explained, "He's about the best piece I've ever had, and I may never see him again."

The officers knew these were, indeed, unusual women, but her reply flabbergasted them.

All but two of the females were armed with sheath or belt-type knives. The officers noted that they were collectively similar in expression, reaction, and communication, and seemed at peace with themselves. Their reaction toward their situation was casual to the point of non-existence. They took off or exchanged clothing in as off-hand a manner as other persons change hats, disrobing and urinating in the presence of the officers like animals. All prisoners gave aliases and it was not until long after their booking at the jail in Independence that their true identities were learned.

The stolen red Toyota was located about two miles northwest of the Myers Ranch, out of gas, and partly covered with brush. It was driven to the Barker Ranch, where Powell, George and Journigan used it to escort the male prisoners down Goler Wash to where the California Highway Patrol vehicles were parked. Early in the evening, Clem, Randy and Soupspoon were booked into the county jail at Independence.

In the afternoon of October 10, Ranger Schneider, located at Anvil Spring, the only place from which radio contact with park headquarters was possible, gave the message that the CHP was having difficulty booking their prisoners at the jail. Sheriff Curtis wasn't anxious to accommodate so many hippies in his jail. Monument Superintendent Robert Murphy Called U.S. District Attorney Duane Keyes in Sacramento. Since some of the arrests were made on federal lands, possibly federal charges could be applied and the prisoners transported to

Sacramento, but Keyes managed to convince the Inyo Sheriff to take them, despite the fact that his other prisoners might object.

Although Inyo County is the second largest in California, at that time its population was only about 16,000. Independence, its county seat, is not the most populace town in the county, although it is rich in history, dating back to its camp of soldiers during the Civil War. It is a small, immaculate town and its county jail is neat and clean, but it lacks the capacity to accommodate a sudden influx of prisoners. The sheriff had had to restrict the accommodation to county prisoners and county officers.

George and Journigan were well-aware of the sheriff's problem, but could not pass up the opportunity to needle the sheriff a bit. When they were asked how many women were being brought in, Journigan replied, "Oh, I guess about twenty women and eight kids." The sheriff turned to his undersheriff and exclaimed, "Where in hell are we gonna put them?" And he asked the patrolman, "What do you think we are running here, a hotel?"

"It's been a long day," George replied. "In fact, about nineteen hours, and we haven't even had anything to eat. Do you mind if we go back to the kitchen and fix a sandwich and a cup of coffee?"

"Hell yes," replied the sheriff in exasperation. "Do anything you want. Help yourselves. I'm getting out of here. I'm going home!"

In searching upper Goler Wash late in the afternoon of October 10, officers found several supply caches. Thirteen sleeping bags were removed from one cache. A U.S. Mail sack marked Miramar was in the possession of Pugh, Morse and Schwarm. A .22-caliber single-shot pistol was in the mail bag, reported as stolen.

From the number of sleeping bags found, it seemed obvious that other members of the Family could be expected to come in. The men agreed that a return to the area in the immediate future was advisable. Other stolen vehicles might also be hidden in the area.

In the four-wheel-drive vehicles of Hailey, Burandt, and Schneider, the women were moved out of the area via the less-difficult Mengel Pass and Butte Valley route where support vehicles had been parked. There remained a sizeable quantity of auto parts, tools, supplies, and personal items at Barker Ranch to be checked out and identified.

Later in the evening, O'Neil, riding in the back of Burandt's pickup, spotted in the vicinity of Mengel Pass the top of a vehicle roll bar in the canyon below. It belonged to a dune buggy that had been driven over the bank and down into the canyon and covered with brush. In this vehicle were found a pair of bolt cutters and a spotting scope. They would later learn the bolt cutters had been used to cut telephone wires at the Sharon Tate house. The spotting scope was probably the

Dune buggies cached at Willow Spring. National Park Service photo.

one Charlie took from Dennis Wilson's house. The dune buggy, reported stolen by the Santa Ana Police Department, was the one Pursell had observed north of Barker Ranch of September 29. The officers lifted and pushed the dune buggy up to the road and Hailey towed it out of the area with his Toyota.

On that same evening of October 10, the CHP officers were preparing to move two stolen dune buggies found in the Willow Springs area. As they approached Anvil Spring just after dark, Hailey and Officer Ben Anderson observed two hippies running up the road toward them. They readily identified themselves as Stephanie Joan Schram, seventeen, an Anaheim Police Department runaway, and Kathryn Rene Lutesinger, also a Los Angeles runaway. Both said they were fleeing from Charlie, the leader of the Family, and that they were afraid for their lives. They had left Barker Ranch the day before and had walked all night and all day. They were relieved to learn that Clem and Randy had been arrested. They knew the two men had been sent to stop them from walking away. They said that Charlie had left the area a couple of days before, and they did not know when he planned to return. Hailey and Steuber were especially interested in Stephanie and Kitty because they appeared to be frightened and willing to talk. Steuber thought they might be a good source of information on the Family.

Upon returning to Lone Pine in the early hours of October 11, Hailey, an expert with recording devices and public address systems, set up his recording equipment and with Steuber interviewed the two young women. Because both were juveniles, it was decided to book them away from the older women who had been taken to the Independence jail.

Steuber was successful in gaining the confidence of Kitty; he was sincerely concerned for her welfare. Kitty, under age, was pregnant by Bobby Beausoleil, a suspect in the murder of Gary Hinman, and afraid for her life. She volunteered considerable information about the Family, but she did not imply that they were involved in criminal activities.

Steuber pursued some sentimental questions concerning her parents and her desires. He urged her to contact her parents, and she finally gave him her mother's telephone number, with the understanding that Steuber would not reveal her present predicament.

Steuber also gained the confidence of Stephanie, who, as a relatively new member of the Family, had less information. Steuber called her parents in Santa Ana, and they agreed to come for her when the officers were in a position to release her.

Kitty's mother in Los Angeles in a telephone interview said, "No, she did not know where her daughter was; yes, she was concerned for her welfare." She told Steuber she was happy to know where her daughter was, but she cautioned Steuber that Kitty was prone to run away and would do so if given the slightest opportunity. Mrs. Lutesinger then revealed that Kitty was wanted by Los Angeles police as a runaway, and that two detectives had been at her home looking for Kitty who, they said, had been a material witness to a homicide. One of the detectives was Sgt. Paul Whitely of the Los Angeles Sheriff's Department, an investigator.

Believing that an early Sunday phone call to the Los Angeles Sheriff's Department would produce nothing but lip service, Steuber nevertheless put in a call for the sheriff's department homicide detail. He asked for Whitely and was advised that the detective was on vacation. When asked if anyone else could help, Steuber briefly stated the situation at Lone Pine and who he had in custody. The officer on the phone listened politely and asked where a return call could be made.

Steuber was concerned about his responsibilities in the case; he had all the formalities to attend to: two young girls in custody, all the paper work, having to contact their parents. But within fifteen minutes the telephone rang in Lone Pine and the caller identified himself as Whitely. Steuber filled him in on the details of the arrest of the two female juveniles. Whitely told him that Kitty Lutesinger was wanted by his department for questioning; her boyfriend, Beausoleil, was presently in jail, a suspect in the murder of Hinman.

He also told Steuber that Kitty was a "rabbit," and would run away at the first opportunity. Whitely said, to Steuber's surprise, that he and his partner would drive to Lone Pine and Independence that day. Whitely and Charles Guenther, accompanied by their wives, arrived at Independence in late afternoon to meet with Steuber and the Inyo County officers.

In questioning seventeen-year-old Kitty, the Los Angeles officers decided they had a knowledgeable witness concerning the Hinman murder in the Topanga Canyon area, and they transported her back to Los Angeles that evening, leaving the others to be interviewed later.

·11·

The Apprehension of Charles Manson

CHP Officer Jim Pursell and Rangers Dick Powell and Earl Curran were enroute to Warm Spring on October 12 to retrieve evidence seized on the October 10 raid. This included gas cans, a tire and a wheel from a dune buggy, a wheel and tire from the 1969 green Ford sedan, a grease gun, and grease cartridges stamped NPS taken from the Michigan loader. The officers had just received information from a couple driving a dune buggy through the area that a white stakebed truck was stuck in the sandy wash between Mengel Pass and Barker Ranch. Knowing this to be the description of one of the stolen vehicles in a possible auto theft ring, additional manpower was requested through the National Park Service at Furnace Creek.

Chief Ranger Leach was at his residence at headquarters when he received Pursell's request for assistance. He called Hailey in Lone Pine and plans were made for Leach and officers he could round up to go through Butte Valley to the Barker ranch. Hailey and his support officers would go through Panamint Valley to the mouth of Goler Wash and be available from that location.

Deputy Sheriff Don Ward at Shoshone called Supt. Murphy and volunteered his services for the raid on Barker Ranch. Use of sheriff's personnel remained a sensitive matter and Murphy suggested Ward obtain approval from the sheriff. Ward's familiarity with the area and with members of the Family made him a valuable recruit for the raid. Undersheriff D. C. Landergren advised Murphy that it was Ward's day off, and he would be on his own and that the federal government should provide insurance coverage for Ward.

Murphy replied, "No problem."

The only other rangers available at the time were Al Schneider and Leach, and they were ready to depart within fifteen minutes. Not much daylight time remained to gather additional support from outlying areas and still arrive at Goler Wash before dark. Ward was instructed to meet them in the Warm Spring area. The officers took shotguns as well as service revolvers, plus ammunition for Powell and Curran.

Proceeding toward Goler Wash, Pursell, Powell and Curran stopped in Butte Valley to talk again to an elderly man, a Mr. Anderson, who had prospected in Death Valley for many years. He lived north of Anvil Spring with his wife and was unwilling to reveal anything of value to the officers. They felt that the Family had in some way instilled fear in the old man.

A little south of Mengel Pass, the officers found the truck stuck in the sand. The truck was a rented vehicle loaded with five barrels of gasoline, a box of groceries, army surplus foul weather gear, women's moccasins, and other items. The officers took the keys and distributor cap and drove off up a side canyon. It was getting late. They parked their 4x4 vehicle about a quarter of a mile north of Barker ranch.

Powell and Pursell walked to a location behind a ridge to the rear and north of the Barker Ranch house. Curran remained with the vehicle to await officers coming in to reinforce the apprehension effort. Powell and Pursell later climbed a ridge to a point above and behind the ranch with Powell having an east view and Pursell a north view of the house. They waited there for Leach, Ward, Schneider and Curran.

They observed four persons, one with a guitar case, walking toward the house from the west, before disappearing from view.

They overheard voices and estimated that there were at least six persons in the house. When the additional officers arrived, a plan of approach to the Barker house was made by radio. Leach made a wide swing across the wash, screened from the house by brush, to a location about two hundred feet to the south. Powell was just off the east side of the building and Curran off to the northwest. Schneider moved up the wash toward the front door. Pursell came off the ridge to the north to a location behind a small outbuilding adjacent to the house and facing the back door.

Suddenly the back door opened and a woman walked into the yard. She had a towel wrapped around her head. She stopped and coughed several times, spat into the dirt, and walked back into the house. It was Diane Bluestein.

Pursell thought, "If she looks up, we're done for."

The back door closed behind her. It was 6:30 p.m. and growing dark rapidly. Ward was close to Pursell's position, and Leach and Schneider were covering the front door. Pursell moved quickly to the back door, flung it open, and for protection moved against the outside wall to the left of the doorway. He ordered all the occupants to hold their positions and place their hands on their heads. There was no response. The order was loudly repeated. A rather slow compliance followed his second order.

Pursell saw a man to his left facing the opposite direction, three women to his left in the kitchen and three other men either sitting or standing around the large kitchen table in the center of the room. Pursell had the men back out to the doorway one at a time with hands on their heads. Each was then passed to the officers who had assembled on the porch outside the back door. After four men were removed from the house, three women were ordered to go out of the house, one at a time, which they did. The men and women followed these orders without comment.

When the kitchen was cleared, Pursell entered the house and picked up a homemade candle burning in a China mug, the only illumination in the now dark building. With it, he conducted a search of the other rooms. He had been in the house before, and was familiar with the floor plan.

He went to the bathroom, which had the usual fixtures but was largely nonfunctional.

He was forced to move the improvised candle around a bit; it made a poor light. He lowered it to the wash basin and a small cupboard below. He observed long hair, like a wig, hanging over the top of the cupboard door, which was partially open. Almost at once, fingers extended through the hair and began to move. Pursell said, "Don't make any false moves." A figure emerged from the cupboard.

As his subject emerged from his cramped quarters, he said with some jocularity that he was glad to be out of the cupboard because it was cramped in there.

The man was clad entirely in buckskin; he looked very different from the others apprehended by the officers. Pursell suspected that this man was the leader of the group, a guy named Charlie. When Pursell asked his name, he replied, "Charles Manson." At that time the last name was of no significance to Pursell, and he assumed it to be an alias.

In Pursell's arrest report he noted that Manson insisted that he was Jesus Christ.

Manson was turned over to the officers outside and Pursell, back inside the house, observed another man identified as William Rex Cole, standing in the bedroom doorway. He also joined the group outside. Later the officers would learn that he was ex-convict David Lee Hamic, a man with more aliases than Charles Manson. Ward and Pursell then made a final search of the house with no further results.

As the officers lined up the subjects along the wall of the house and systematically searched them, there came an ear-shattering boom. Everyone froze, waiting for some clarification. Ward, in attempting to close a door, had accidentally discharged a shotgun he was carrying. Dust and dirt drifted down on the silent male subjects lined up against the wall, but the only casualty was a hole through the broom leaning against the inside wall of the kitchen.

As Ward came out on the back porch, one of the girls asked him what had happened. Ward, a bit embarrassed but with some humor, replied, "Oh, one of them lipped off to me, so I let him have it."

From the time Pursell opened the back door until the suspects were all apprehended, only ten minutes passed. Pursell informed the nine subjects assembled in the back yard that they were under arrest for grand theft, arson, and grand theft auto. A second thorough search was conducted on the six men, who were ordered to strip down to their shorts. A couple of sheath knives were found, as well as knives that were on the kitchen table. No firearms were found, but darkness prevented a search of the house and outbuildings. There was little conversation. Manson asked, "Which one of you guys is Powell?" Powell was surprised Manson knew his name. Manson told him that the group in Jail Canyon had reported that he treated them well.

Those arrested were Charles Milles Manson, thirty-three, also known as Jesus Christ; Bruce McGregor Davis, twenty-seven, also known as Bruce McMillan; William Rex Cole, thirty-four, true name David Lee Hamic; Larry Jones, nineteen, true name Lawrence Charles Bailey; Scott Bell Davis, seventeen, true name Kenneth Richard Brown; Christopher Jesus, twenty, true name John Phillip Haught, known in the Family as Zero; Beth Tracy, nineteen, true name Collie Sinclair; Diane Elizabeth Bluestein, sixteen, true name Diane Elizabeth Lake, and Sherry Andrews, twenty, true name Claudia Leigh Smith.

Others participating in the raid on October 12 approached Goler Wash from the west traveling down through the floor of Panamint Valley. Leach had advised Hailey about 2 p.m. on October 12 that another group of hippies was in Goler Wash. CHP Officers Manning and Anderson, accompanied by Lt. Jerry Fleming of the sheriff's office, were immediately dispatched to secure the mouth of Goler Wash in Panamint Valley. Hailey, with U.S. Forest Service Ranger Ben Casad, were instructed to follow and meet the other officers there as soon as possible.

Late in the afternoon, burning up the road across the salt flat about four miles south of Ballarat, the men were heading out. Anderson was driving the cage patrol cruiser; Fleming was in the back and Manning was in the right front. They were told to stop anyone going or coming into Goler Wash. All of a sudden they spotted a dune buggy coming at them real fast with dust flying. Anderson hit the brakes and slipped the outfit broadside on the dirt road. Manning bailed out on the right side, spitting dirt, as the car blocked the road. Manning racked a round into the riot gun he was carrying. He could hear Fleming yelling in the back of the car because he couldn't get out; the back door handles inside had been removed for transporting prisoners. Manning let him out with his tommy gun and as the air cleared, they beheld an elderly couple with a startled poodle in the driver's lap. They faced the patrol car with concerned looks on their faces. The old people had been trying out the dune buggy with the intent to purchase it. The officers apologized, explained their situation, and went on toward Goler Wash, the men on edge.

Hailey and Casad arrived about 6:30 p.m. at the mouth of Goler Wash. They had just settled in when they saw a vehicle approaching from the north. It turned into Goler Wash and was stopped by Hailey and Casad. It was driven by Patti Sue Jardin, whose true name was Catherine Gillies. She was accompanied by Susan Phyllis Bartell, known in the Family as Country Sue. They told the officers that they had left two sleeping bags and some wine in a cave up Goler Wash the night before. They said, "We got scared when it got dark and went to a hotel in Barstow to spend the night." They said they were going back up to spend the night in Goler Wash.

They gave the officers permission to look into the trunk of their car. It was full of grocery goods, neither boxed or sacked. The girls denied knowing anyone who might be in the Goler Wash or Barker Ranch area. They offered their purses for inspection.

In Jardin's purse was a Gulf Travel Card, which she said was given to her, but which was reported as stolen. She had used the credit card to rent a motel room and buy gasoline in Barstow, stating she signed the purchase slips as Penelope something or other; she knew a check would be run on it. The credit card had the name of J. C. Relles imprinted on it. Susan Bartell's purse contained an ID card belonging to William Rex Cole, who was arrested at Barker Ranch that same day, October 12. Bartell's purse also contained a Barstow Holiday Inn key to room 216, a list of forty names and telephone numbers, possibly a hate sheet, and a list of fourteen food stores and their locations. Further checking revealed a letter and a check for thirty-five dollars made to Sandy Good by her father. Sandy was arrested at the Barker Ranch October 10 under her married name, Sandy Pugh.

In the glove compartment were three shotgun shells. Under the front seat was a brown leather wallet with an ID card belonging to Diane Marie Von Ahn. Also in the vehicle were two letters to Lynne Fromme, care of Spahn Ranch, Chatsworth. Both of these women were arrested at the Barker Ranch. The names had little meaning for the officers but Spahn Ranch gave them a tie-in with the stolen dune buggies.

In the vehicle was a letter addressed to Mr. Charles Manson who, at this time, October 12, was being apprehended by other officers at Barker Ranch. Also in the car was an envelope containing a statement from Robert K. Beausoleil to H. Fignslie revealing circumstances of what appeared to have ended in murder and a contract on a 1969 Ford rental car, the one found on Hunter Mountain September 19. The contract was made on a credit card signed by Penelope Tracy. The automobile in which the women were traveling was a 1958 Oldsmobile registered to Phillip J. Bartell of Canoga Park.

Both of the girls had been in the area before and were bringing in a supply of food to the Barker Ranch. Obviously connected with stolen cars, credit cards, and other property, they were arrested and detained until transportation could arrive.

At Barker Ranch the officers started walking their subjects down to the two 4x4 Park Service pickups. Most of them were loaded in the back of one pickup while the others followed to provide light. Manson noticed the ranger uniforms and asked, "How come you guys are hassling me? You should be out telling people about the flowers and animals." He could understand the CHP and the sheriff's deputies arresting him, but he thought it inappropriate for park rangers to be involved.

The officers were of the opinion that Manson, Hamic, and two others, possibly Brown and Jesus, had just arrived at Barker Ranch after walking up Goler Wash. Davis and possibly Bailey had just returned from Las Vegas earlier and had stalled in the sand. Pursell believed they were in the house discussing what had happened on October 10. Contrary to some reports, they did not fully realize the extent of previous arrests.

Ward and Pursell stood on the rear bumper of the lead pickup and kept the arrested persons under surveillance. Near the Lotus mine, Manson requested a stop so he could pick up a pack sack he had left beside the road; he had left an expensive guitar in the pack. He asked to be let out of the pickup to look for the pack, but his request was denied. Park Service personnel later found the missing pack and entered it as evidence.

The pickups continued on down the wash. During the ride Manson demonstrated the influence he exerted over the group. At least twice he made statements that caused the others to say "Amen" two or three times in unison. On occasions when the others become involved in whispered, giggly conversations, Charlie simply looked at them and immediately they fell silent. The stare produced results without a word being spoken.

As planned, the officers gave no instructions to their prisoners in the field as to the rights under the law, and no questions were asked. On the trip down the canyon, Manson said that white people ruin the land and God's creatures, which he and his followers did not do. He said that the black people were going to take over the country and that he and his group was only trying to find peace and a quiet place, but the officers were the Establishment and would not leave them alone. He warned the officers that they were in deep trouble; they were white and cops, a double jeopardy. "You should escape while you have the chance," he said.

At the first of several dry-rock falls, the passengers were unloaded and walked over the difficult terrain for several miles. Ward, Pursell, Powell and Curran, guarding them, took one 4x4 vehicle and started the slow, tedious journey in the dark night. They were to be met at the mouth of Goler Wash by other officers from Panamint Valley. Rangers Leach and Schneider had left the party at the top of the rock falls and headed back toward Furnace Creek.

Hailey and other officers posted at the mouth of Goler Wash had not expected the arrival of the two women suspects, Jardin and Bartell. They could not communicate word of their encounter with the officers at Barker Ranch. There arose the possibility that even more suspects were moving about the desert in order to prevent apprehension. Hailey and Highway Patrolman Anderson handcuffed the two women to the cruiser and remained in the area where the vehicles were parked.

Manning, Fleming and Casad hiked up the Wash for about a mile to a point where the canyon is very narrow, and they could detect anyone hiking up or down. Casad had a riot gun, and Manning and Fleming each had a Tommy gun.

It was dark in that canyon, and the men couldn't see a thing. Not wanting to reveal their positions by using flashlights they sat it out, wondering if the guys at Barker Ranch would be coming their way. Maybe they'd encountered a situation that had altered their plans. The men sat, listening to the night sounds, the crickets, a night bird and innumerable sounds they couldn't even identify.

All of a sudden they could hear voices and see an occasional flash of light that appeared to be moving down the canyon. Both Fleming and Manning cocked their Tommy guns, but Casad said he couldn't get his shotgun cocked. Whoever was coming down the canyon was almost upon them, and Manning grabbed Casad's gun and cocked it for him.

About then Fleming said, "Let's do it." They were about 25 or 30 yards away, and they jumped out from behind the rocks and yelled, "Hold it!" All they could see were eight or nine shadows with possibly a flashlight behind them.

Then Don Ward, a deputy with the Barker Ranch group, yelled, "Don't shoot, it's us."

The men were relieved. They were glad nothing had happened because there could have been some people shot out there on the very dark desert that night.

The suspects were led on down to the mouth of the wash where the vehicles were parked. It was 11 p.m. and the suspects seemed tired. They were asked to sit in a circle and relax. The girls said they were hungry so some of the officers opened up U.S. Forest Service boxed rations and fed them. As the girls began eating, Manson started staring at them, and they immediately spit out the food into the dirt.

Manson asked Manning, "Is that a Tommy gun you are carrying?" He then smiled and said, "You wouldn't shoot me, would you?"

Manning pointed the gun at Charlie and said, "Get up off your butt and take off, and we'll find out."

He gave Manning a dirty look and turned away.

Manning made another effort to instill a little respect into the group. Within their hearing range, he asked Hailey if he could take Charlie "for a little walk. There's a vertical mine shaft over that way," he explained, pointing, "and we can drop him down it and save everyone a lot of time and money."

Manning, of course, was not even remotely aware of what would eventually unfold and the prophetic nature of his remarks.

By midnight, the last of the suspects was loaded and headed for the Inyo County jail at Independence 125 miles away. None of the individuals apprehended demonstrated violence or intent of violence; they seemed passively indifferent about being arrested. They were viewed as a pathetic, cruddy, vile group of young people having no visible purpose or direction in life. They appeared so diminutive and young, like runaway children, with their filthy clothes, smelly bodies, and a degenerated vocabulary. Many exhibited retarded or stuporous reactions, which the officers suspected were the result of prolonged use of drugs.

The officers felt that specific individuals among the number, including Charlie, if given the opportunity, might give one the silent death treatment with a sharp knife, but the others seemed so unconventional and lacking in any criminal intent that the officers felt frustrated and somewhat puzzled in handling them. Auto theft, credit card theft, and arson charges were yet to be filed against them in the Inyo court. They hadn't really looked like arsonists or car thieves as they lounged in the dirt and cradled babies in front of Barker Ranch in Death Valley.

·12·
The Pieces of the Puzzle Fall Together

On October 12 at the San Dimas Sheriff's Station, Kitty Lutesinger told investigators details relating to the murder of Gary Hinman. She told them of conversations she had had with Family members at Barker Ranch. One such conversation was of special interest to the officers. Sadie Mae Glutz told Kitty she had had a fight with a man who pulled her hair, and that she had stabbed him several times in the legs. Lutesinger's statement puzzled Whitely and Guenther. The story seemed to have a discrepancy. There was another possible consideration, however. Hinman hadn't been stabbed in the legs, but Voytek Frykowski, in the Tate murders, had.

Law enforcement people now knew that Sadie Mae Glutz was arrested at Barker Ranch under the name of Donna Mae Powell and they would later learn that her true name was Susan Denise Atkins. The next morning the officers flew to Independence to talk to her. Patrolman George took the Los Angeles officers to Lone Pine, so crowded was the jail in Independence, to interrogate her. At the Sportsman Cafe, over a sweet roll and coffee, she was amenable to talking.

She admitted that she and Beausoleil had been to Hinman's house and that Beausoleil had pulled a knife and slashed Hinman's face when he refused to give them money. At no point did she implicate Manson. She said they had stayed in Hinman's house for two days to prevent him from sleeping, and told how Beausoleil finished Hinman when she was in another room. She also indicated she knew something of the murder of Shorty Shea at Spahn Ranch. She said she only told the officers what she thought they already knew, and she refused to have her statements taped. The identity of "Mary," who had been at Hinman's house, remained a mystery.

Marnie Kay Reeves, arrested at Barker Ranch, had had a prior arrest under the name of Mary Scott, and officers would later learn that her true name was Patricia Krenwinkel. Kitty had said that Mary was a slim redhead. The only slim redhead in the jail at Independence was arrested as Elizabeth Elaine Williamson, true name Lynette Alice Fromme. Much later she attempted to assassinate President Gerald Ford.

The Los Angeles officers decided to seek the release of all three girls as witnesses or suspects in the murder. At the Pines Cafe in Independence, Whitely and Guenther conferred with District Attorney Frank Fowles. "We believe you have something here more than just auto theft," they told him. "'We're quite certain some of these people were involved in the Hinman murder and in the Tate murders.''

They took Susan Atkins by air back to Ontario to the San Dimas Sheriff's Station near Pomona and booked her on suspicion of murder.

The next day, Whitely and Guenther drove back to Independence to attempt to determine others who may have been in the Hinman residence at the time he was killed, but interrogation of the jailed Family members failed to yield any further evidence. Relying on Kitty Lutesinger's comments, they returned to Los Angeles with Marnie Kay Reeves and Elizabeth Elaine Williamson as suspects and witnesses to murder. The deputies learned from Marnie whose true name was Patricia Krenwinkel, that the other woman at the Hinman house was Mary Brunner. She was an early Family member, perhaps even the first one. She had been convicted of credit card forgery and was in jail in Los Angeles during the Tate-LaBianca murders. She evidently did not go to Death Valley, but upon her release from jail went to her home in Wisconsin with her child, Valentine Michael Manson.

The Inyo County officers had no charges against Marnie Kay Reeves (Patricia Krenwinkel), the "Katie" who stabbed and stabbed at both the Tate and LaBianca murders. A few days after her release, she flew to the home of her aunt, Mrs. Reeves, in Mobile, Alabama. Squeaky Fromme, also released, returned to Inyo County to be near and, if possible, aid Charlie Manson.

On learning that Kitty Lutesinger was willing to give additional information on stolen vehicles, Dave Steuber spent seven hours interviewing her at the San Dimas Sheriff's Station in Los Angeles. She told him of stolen vehicles that had not yet been recovered and also that Manson, Christopher Jesus, Mino Minette, Diane Bluestein and Rachel Morse were responsible for the burning of the Michigan loader. She identified suspects in the embezzlement of the 1969 Ford from Hertz and identified persons who stole various dune buggies and the red Toyota. She also had much to say about burglaries, armed robberies, dope operations, and various other crimes involving the Family.

On October 14, Pursell and Powell drove to Indian Ranch in Panamint Valley to talk to Arlene Barker, owner of the Barker Ranch. She said she had only limited knowledge of the character of Charles Manson. He had come to her home at Indian Ranch a year and a half before to ask permission to camp at her place at Goler Wash. She next saw him a few months later when he brought her a framed gold record which had been presented to the Beach Boys by Capitol Records. He had indicated that he was an arranger or composer of one of the selections on the album. She was not impressed, but she kept the gold album.

The last time she had seen him was about three weeks before his arrest when he came to Indian Ranch and proposed to purchase Barker Ranch. She had been agreeable to the purchase if he could produce cash for payment, but he had said he would see her later.

She reported that on his last visit Charlie had appeared very scroungy, filthy dirty, with a long beard, quite different from the first time she had seen him. He was driving a dune buggy and was accompanied by another hippie, equally dirty. Manson indicated they were filming a movie around Olancha. She told the officers she had not given anyone permission to remain at her ranch for an extended period of time, but because of its remoteness, she had little control of those who passed through or camped there.

District Attorney Fowles called Death Valley National Monument Superintendent Robert Murphy and his chief ranger, Leach, on October 14. He was anxious to send someone to Barker Ranch as soon as possible because he had information from Los Angeles authorities that possibly two men and one woman had been murdered and were buried in the Barker Ranch area. He also wanted to check for firearms and other personal property, hoping they might contribute to the evidence in upcoming court action.

The Park Service long-wheel-base vehicles had taken a considerable beating on the previous trips, and were unavailable. Fowles, who understood the problem, agreed to furnish a county Ford Bronco, one of the best of the vehicles for such terrain, and sent a mosquito control district employee with the Bronco to meet Murphy, Leach, and Powell in Goler Wash.

As they were traveling up the alluvial fan toward the mouth of Goler, Murphy said to the driver, "Maybe you'd better put this thing in four-wheel-drive."

"This vehicle is pretty capable, and I think it will be OK without it," he'd replied.

As they approached the first rock fall, the driver exclaimed, "You mean we drive up over that thing?"

Murphy and Powell nodded and said in unison, "That's the way we go."

The driver said, "This thing will never make it over that; I'm not going up there."

Murphy suggested that he let Powell, who was used to the terrain, drive.

The driver replied, "It's your neck, but I'll walk." After three or four dry rock falls, the county employee was positive the Park Service people were out of their minds, but he rode from Lotus Mine to Barker Ranch in the back seat, exhausted from the walk.

At the ranch they found a guitar, Cathy Gillies' purse, a sizeable food supply, and other items that indicated the Family intended to stay at the ranch all winter. Their inventory included fourteen cartons of candy bars, eight large rolls of cheese, four gallons of peanut butter, three gallons of honey, five half-gallon jars of jam, two half gallons of jelly, five huge boxes of crackers, three boxes of graham crackers, two cases of canned milk, forty gallons of wheat germ, corn meal and flour, and four large cans of smoking tobacco. There were other items in small quantities but not much variety. They also found many items of clothing, mostly women's.

The bathroom where Pursell had apprehended Manson from under the wash basin was inspected. It was filthy. The toilet was full of urine and water only dripped into the rusted holding tank.

"You could probably flush this thing only once every twenty-four hours," Leach observed.

There was not much furniture in the front room or in the bedroom. A king-size mattress so dirty even a dog would shun it was in the middle of the front room floor. Someone had defecated in the corner of the living room. An interesting pincushion was found by Murphy. The stitches were cut and inside was a buckskin bag containing an amber or cream-colored powder. The rangers speculated it was a cheap form of heroin, Mexican brown, prized by the Family for a special event. It was turned over to the sheriff's office for analysis. There it disappeared, and it was never seen again.

In the bunkhouse the officers found leather-working tools. Of special interest were twenty-four loaded .45-caliber cartridges commonly used in a handgun found on a bench. No such firearms were observed by arresting officers nor were the shotguns observed September 29 north of Barker Ranch found. In the bunkhouse and an adjacent shed were found tools and equipment, even an acetylene welding outfit, normally found in an automotive repair shop.

The officers searched areas where soil had been disturbed and dug a three-and-a-half-foot trench across the bonfire ritual area where Kitty Lutesinger had indicated Manson held sessions of Satanic worship, drug use and sex orgies. There was no evidence of a grave at this location.

There was a report that Charlie and Tex Watson had taken a girl for a walk and after being gone for less than an hour, returned without her. She was never seen again.

The only living thing observed at Barker ranch by the officers was one chicken, obviously lonesome.

Camping areas in the vicinity were checked out and places leveled for sleeping bags were found, but there was no indication of burials. The lookout post on the hill south of the ranch was checked and proved to be quite a nest. Dirt covered its tin roof, and inside was a dirty mattress. The toilet area was just about any place outside. Another rock-ringed lookout contained a field telephone and a ground line leading toward Barker Ranch.

The officers checked the nearby Myers Ranch. This location had obviously been cleaned up. The floors were neat and the bed made with the bedspread carefully tucked over the top. No Family items were found. Charlie told the arresting officers that the Family avoided the Myers Ranch because "the ghost of Bill Myers still lived there."

North of Myers Ranch, the officers located the site where three women and two babies had been found. A filthy canvas indicated the occupants had not even left the bedding site to relieve themselves. They also found an area where desert flora had been destroyed in the Family's practice of Rommel desert tactics. The girls had told the officers about Charlie forcing them to dig fortresses far into the night. The officers searched for graves but found none.

The officers believed their search had been unrewarding and they returned down Goler Wash with everyone walking at the dry rock falls except Powell, the driver. The county mosquito abatement man shielded his eyes; he believed Powell and the Bronco were about to take an end-over-end roll into the canyon below.

On October 16 another very thorough check was made of Goler Wash with Sgt. Hailey in charge. It included all the agencies that had been there before plus the Los Angeles Sheriff's Office, homicide and auto theft teams. Dune buggies and additional food caches were found. Each of the stolen vehicles had been camouflaged by various means, with sagebrush, willows and camouflaged parachutes. License plates had been removed or changed. Tire tracks had been obliterated by brushing them out with shrubs. In one instance a rock wall had been built across tracks leading to two dune buggies. Food and supply caches were usually in holes lined with canvas and the top covered with vegetation. Two of the dune buggies had been repainted in natural desert colors.

Lutesinger had revealed that Charlie told the girls that if one or two officers entered the area, they were to attack the officers with their knives and try to inflict facial cuts or cut off an ear. If a large group of officers entered the area, the girls were to do all sorts of crazy things, such as disrobing and urinating in front of them. In the event officers were killed, their uniforms were to be put on posts on Goler Wash and Mengel Pass to ward off future entry of officers into the area. The officers believed that the girls had been attempting to comply with this strategy of Manson's when they encountered them at Barker Ranch.

·13·
On the Lookout

After Dave Steuber returned from Los Angeles, fourteen suspects were arraigned in Inyo County on twenty charges of arson, grand theft auto, receiving stolen property, and possession of illegal firearms, notably a sawed-off shotgun. The fourteen suspects were held for a total bail of $262,500, including Charlie's $12,000 for arson and $25,000 for possession of stolen property.

The true names of many of those held were not known to Inyo County authorities at the time charges were filed in the justice court or even later during the preliminary hearings. Some suspects had no identification; others had false identification. Several were juveniles and most had not been previously fingerprinted. Many were released and only much later were their true names to be learned. Some had been involved in other crimes unknown to Inyo officers, and within a short time, attempts were made to relocate some of the suspects in the Death Valley area. It came as a terrible shock to the Inyo officers when the vicious record of the Family, in the Tate-LaBianca and Gary Hinman murders, came out into the open. It was hard to believe that the Family whose members the arresting officers had first viewed only as unkempt, irresponsible hippies, had committed these hideous crimes. Death Valley could well have had its own blood bath, had the officers provided the opportunity.

In November, Inyo law enforcement officials were warned to be on the lookout for Manson Family members who may have returned to the desert. Tex Montgomery and Bruce Davis were reported by Las Vegas informants to have been seen driving a blue panel Volkswagen. Davis was now a suspect in the Hinman homicide and the shooting of Christopher Jesus. Montgomery was now a suspect in the Tate-LaBianca murders.

Charles Sorrells, a businessman in Shoshone and an old desert hand, was driving his four-wheel-drive vehicle near Barker Ranch on November 23 when he noticed two hippie males sitting on the hillside above the Barker buildings. Sorrells had been quite well informed about the investigations and when he returned home, called the Los Angeles Sheriff's Department to report his observations. On November 26, Los Angeles Sheriff's Lieutenant Grimm and 13 deputies arrived at Furnace

Creek with three large four-wheel-drive vehicles. They requested assistance from the Park Service in guiding them into the Goler Wash area. Grimm wanted to arrive at Barker Ranch before dark that evening.

As the trip from Furnace Creek to Barker Ranch required about four hours of slow, hazardous driving, the arrival time was changed to dawn of November 27. The officers, accompanied by Superintendent Murphy, took the Warm Spring road into Butte Valley. They arrived at Anderson Camp* as dawn was breaking and were surprised to find that the Anderson's were not there. They cautiously checked the outbuildings and a couple of old trailer houses. Anderson's vehicle and his dog were nowhere to be found. The five barrels of gasoline on the stolen Chevrolet truck which Powell and Pursell had found stuck in the sand were stored there. There was some apprehension that Family members had returned, killed or driven off the Andersons, and were hidden out in the area.

Grimm split his force of deputies into pairs for convergence on the Myers and Barker ranches. Four would be taken by vehicle to Willow Spring to hike about four miles south to the Myers Ranch. Others went to Anvil Spring to check out the cabin there and then hike over Mengel Pass to Barker Ranch. Grimm, a sergeant, and Murphy were to check out Redlands Canyon and then return to meet a Los Angeles Sheriff's Department helicopter in mid-morning at Anvil Spring. Inyo County Deputy Dennis Cox with two Los Angeles deputies were to come into Goler Wash by Wingate Wash.

Before the deputies left, Grimm showed them mug shots of Charles Denton Watson and Bruce Davis, the murder suspects being sought. The officers, armed with semi-automatic rifles, and obviously new to the force, expressed some concern.

"Lieutenant," one of them asked Grimm, "how do you want us to respond if we are fired on?"

Grimm, a giant of a man, six-foot-five, scowled and replied, "Shoot the bastards. They are murder suspects aren't they?"

The sun was just coming up as Grimm and his two companions hiked over a low ridge in approaching the Panamint Russ's property. No one had been living there. The officers spaced themselves about 200 yards apart. They heard a dog bark so they waited on the ridge. Finally the front door of the house opened and an elderly man clad in long underwear stepped into the yard. Then an elderly woman stuck her head out of the door, and Murphy recognized the couple as the Andersons. The officers called out to ask if there were others there and received a negative reply.

---

* Author's Note: In the desert community most places are known by surname only.

The officers then descended from the ridge for a talk with the Andersons. Grimm showed them the pictures of Watson and Davis. The old man seemed nervous, looking at the sky and then down at his feet. He said he had never seen two fellows that looked like that. The Andersons provided little information. They claimed they didn't know anything about the gas barrels either.

The officers returned to Anvil Spring and in a short time, the helicopter arrived with Park Ranger Paul Fodor and a Los Angeles deputy sheriff. The officers in the helicopter had checked both the Myers and Barker ranches and had seen no suspects. Grimm asked if there were other areas that should be searched. Murphy suggested they fly over to the Harry Briggs place on the west side of the Panamints to see if he had seen anyone in the area. The old man was cutting wood as they landed, and he never even looked up or quit sawing as they landed. Murphy and the sergeant, both carrying rifles, walked right up to Briggs before he looked up and spoke to them. He said he hadn't seen those characters around his place for a long time. Manson had tried to rent a couple of his cabins about a year before.

"That son of a bitch knows better than to come up here," Briggs said with some vehemence.

He continued sawing wood with his handsaw and didn't look up as they took off.

"Christ," the sergeant commented, "Way out here, isolated in these mountains, you'd think the old guy was on the corner of Hollywood and Vine! Traffic sure don't bother him."

The officers flew back to Anvil Spring and then to Barker Ranch where they met the search teams. One of the Los Angeles deputies mentioned Tenerellie, who had been found shot in a Bishop motel room on October 2. The deputies had learned that Tenerellie was known to the Family; they called him Dago.

The search terminated when no further evidence had been found. With a sigh of relief, the whole contingent of officers headed home.

·14·
Murderers in Custody

The drama of the Manson Family left Inyo County and Death Valley when the Los Angeles Police Department and the Los Angeles Sheriff's Department finally pieced together enough evidence to file charges against the hippies, whose custody they had botched in the Spahn Ranch raid. The persons responsible for the Tate-LaBianca murders, with no credit to Los Angeles law enforcement, were safely lodged in the Inyo County jail. All Los Angeles county and city had to do was come and get them. A small handful of brave officers had risked their necks to corral the Manson Family.

When the Family members were sent off to Los Angeles to face charges of homicide, Inyo County gave a sigh of relief and figuratively said, "Thank God!" The lack of jury trials probably saved the county over half a million dollars in taxes, which its citizens could ill afford.

In November, 1969, Los Angeles District Attorney Evelle Younger assigned his deputies, Vincent Bugliosi and Aaron Stovitz, to the Manson case. Gathering evidence was difficult, but even more incomprehensible was the task of finding a motive where none seemed to exist.

So urgent was their need for evidence in this case that Bugliosi, with five Los Angeles Police Department officers, arrived in Independence at 1:30 a.m. on the morning of November 19, to meet with District Attorney Fowles, his deputy, Buck Gibbens, and special investigator Jack Gardiner. Later that day they made a hurried trip up Goler Wash to Barker Ranch to look for clues that might tie in to the Tate-LaBianca murders. The green bus, disabled at Barker, had women's clothing, shoes, magazines, and trash covering the floor. They gathered up many items to be transported back to Los Angeles, but the trip also taught them the hazards of Goler Wash.

While files in Inyo County provided much information that would aid in preparation for the trials in Los Angeles, Bugliosi learned very little from interrogation of the women still held in jail—Leslie, Ouisch, Snake, Brenda and Gypsy. He interviewed Squeaky Fromme and Sandra

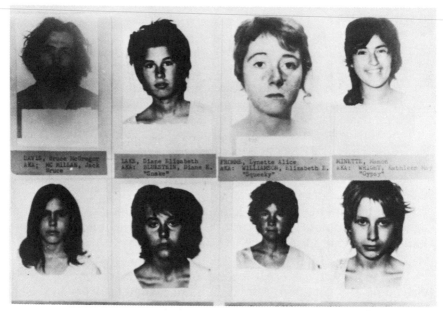

Mug Shots: Top, left to right—Bruce Davis, Diane Lake, Lynette (Squeaky) Fromme, Catherine (Gypsy), Share. Bottom, left to right—Ruth Ann Morehouse, Nancy Pitman (known as Brenda McCann), Sandra Good, Catherine Gilles (known as Patti Sue Jardin).

Good, who were hanging around town in order to be close to Charlie. Bugliosi saw Manson escorted from jail to the courtroom for arraignment on the National Park Service Michigan loader arson charge. He found it difficult to believe that these people could have been involved in the murders in which they were implicated.

Susan Atkins, confined in Sybil Brand jail for women in Los Angeles, had related the gruesome details of the Tate-LaBianca murders to inmates Ronnie Howard and Virginia Graham. On November 17, having heard from Ronnie Howard, investigative officers went to Sybil Brand jail to interview Graham. They learned enough to convince them the case was solved, but proof was still elusive. Officers learned other details of the Tate-LaBianca, Shea and Gary Hinman murders from Danny DeCarlo.

When the media were on the telephone to Inyo County and Park Service authorities late in November to attempt to establish a relationship between the Death Valley escapades and the Los Angeles County murders, the Inyo County officers were not in a position to support their contentions. Pressure mounted in Los Angeles for the airing of a solution to the horrible murders. The press, at the request of the

Mug Shots: Top, left to right—Manson, Tex Watson, Clem Grogan, Bill Vance. Bottom, left to right—Leslie Van Houten, Mary Brunner, Linda Kasabian, and Susan Atkins (known as Sadie Mae Glutz).

prosecution, refrained from airing the details at its disposal. Tex Watson was still in Texas fighting extradition, and Linda Kasabian and Marnie Reeves had yet to be located.

In late November the press descended on Independence and Death Valley en masse. A television crew came by helicopter to film Goler Wash and Barker Ranch. Jim Pursell was in demand as the person who had snatched Charlie Manson by his long hair from under the bathroom cabinet. Ranger Dick Powell was also interviewed about his part in the capture of the Family. All of this attention was difficult for the Inyo officials, because the Los Angeles authorities had not yet obtained sufficient information, nor had they issued complaints for the arrest of all of those suspected of involvement in the murders. The tension rose between the two law enforcement agencies.

In December, police learned that Marnie Reeves was actually Patricia Krenwinkel, also known as Katie. On information received from her father in Inglewood, she was arrested in Mobile, Alabama. Early in December, Linda Kasabian turned herself in to police in Concord, New Hampshire, after learning that she was wanted as a participant in the Tate murders.

On December 1, Los Angeles Chief of Police Edward M. Davis faced a host of reporters and cameramen to announce the department had solved the Tate case. Warrants had been issued for Charles D. (Tex) Watson, 24, who was then in custody in Texas, and Linda Kasabian, whose whereabouts were not then known. Davis said that indictments would be issued for four or five more persons, but the names of Charles Manson and Susan Atkins were not mentioned. Davis also said, to the surprise of the reporters, that the Tate and LaBianca murders were linked, something the press had suspected but was unable to impress on either the Tate or LaBianca investigators. Davis did not mention that it had taken the Los Angeles Police Department two months to follow up on information that had been provided by the sheriff's department the day after the Tate murders.

The long trials began in Los Angeles, demanding the law enforcement many hours of investigative reporting and extensive periods of time on the witness stand. An outcome of this was that Mary Brunner was given immunity in exchange for her testimony in the murder of Gary Hinman, whose fatal stabbing by Robert Beausoleil she had witnessed. Beausoleil, on the stand in his own defense, fingered Manson as the murderer, but Mary Brunner did everything she could to absolve Charlie of responsibility. Beausoleil received the death penalty. In other proceedings, Susan Atkins pleaded guilty in the Hinman murder and was given life imprisonment.

In the trials for the murders of Hinman and Shea, Charles Manson, Bruce Davis, and Steve Grogan were tried separately. Manson and Davis received life sentences. Grogan's jury recommended death, but the judge decided that he was too stupid and too hopped-up on drugs to make his own decisions, and declared that it was Charlie who decided who lived and who died, Grogan was given life.

Manson, Krenwinkel, Atkins and Leslie Van Houten were found guilty in the Tate-LaBianca trial, including seven counts of murder and varying counts of conspiracy to commit murder. In sentencing the guilty persons, Judge Older pointed out that "considering the stark fact that seven lives were snuffed out by total strangers, the death sentence was not only appropriate but almost compelled by the circumstances." It was the longest murder trial in American history, and cost nearly a million dollars. Tex Watson was tried separately, found guilty and sentenced to death.

But in June of 1972, the United States Supreme Court ruled that the death penalty, under certain circumstances, constituted cruel and unusual punishment. The entire Manson Family was off Death Row and given life imprisonment.

·15·
The Family Carries on with a Vengeance

The arrest and conviction of Charles Milles Manson and various members of his notorious Family did not end the fear and anxiety in Los Angeles County and the desert area of Inyo County. By no means had all of the Manson cult been imprisoned, and there was abundant evidence during the long trial of Charlie, Tex and others that those who were free were still very loyal to their leader and the Family. Drugs and violence did not cease all at once.

On November 3, 1969, the body of a young woman was found over an embankment at Mulholland and Bowmont Drive in almost the same spot where Marina Habe's body had been found. A brunette in her late teens, she had been stabbed one hundred and fifty-seven times. Ruby Pearl remembered seeing her with the Family at the Spahn Ranch and thought her name was Sherry. A Sherry Ann Cooper had fled Barker Ranch with Barbara Hoyt and fortunately was still alive. A Sherry Andrews (Claudia Leigh Smith) was among the twenty-six persons arrested at Barker Ranch in October. The identity of the Mulholland victim is still unknown, but the proximity of the time of her death with that of Zero suggests that she may have been present at the murder and was killed so she wouldn't talk.

On November 21, the bodies of James Sharp, fifteen, and Doreen Gaul, nineteen, were found in a downtown Los Angeles alley. They had been killed elsewhere, stabbed over fifty times with a long-bladed knife or bayonet. Both were Scientologists and Doreen was reportedly a former girlfriend of the Manson Family member Bruce Davis, also a Scientologist, who had disappeared shortly after being questioned in the death of Zero.

Joel Dean Pugh, husband of Family member Sandra Good, was found in a London hotel room with his throat slit December 1. London police ruled the death a suicide, but when Inyo County District Attorney Frank

Fowles learned of the death, he made official inquiries through Interpol to check the visa of Bruce Davis to see if he was in London at the time. Officials reported that Davis had been in London in April and had been there more recently, but they had no official record. He had been in Los Angeles in February of 1970, when he was questioned in Inyo County on auto theft charges and then released. After he was indicted by the grand jury in the Hinman murder, he disappeared again, not surfacing again until December 2, 1970, four days after the mysterious disappearance of Defense Attorney Ronald Hughes. After Sandra Good and Lynette Fromme vacated a motel room in Independence, authorities found a letter from an unidentified Family member stating, "I do not want what happened to Joel to happen to me."

Barbara Hoyt had reluctantly agreed to testify in the Tate-LaBianca trial, but she left home unexpectedly after receiving a death threat. In September she was contacted by some of the Manson women and offered a free trip to Hawaii in lieu of testifying at the trial. She accepted. Those who persuaded her to leave were Clem, Squeaky, Gypsy, and Ouisch. With Ouisch, whose true name was Ruth Ann Morehouse, Barbara went to Hawaii, remaining at a hotel for several days, during which Ouisch seldom let her go out, telling her the police would be looking for her.

After several days, Ouisch told Barbara she had to go back to California but that Barbara was to remain in Hawaii. The women took a cab to the airport where Ouisch encouraged Barbara to order a hamburger; while Barbara paid the check, Ouisch took the hamburger outside and reportedly laced it with the equivalent of ten tabs of LSD. While Barbara ate it, Ouisch bade her farewell and boarded her flight.

Barbara became high, then ill and panicky. She started running and collapsed near the Salvation Army headquarters. Byron Galloway, an employee of the state hospital who specialized in drug abuse, observed her plight and took her to Queens Medical Center, where her condition was diagnosed as acute psychosis, drug induced. Police, finding her identification on her person, called her father, who flew to Hawaii and returned her to Los Angeles. Bravely, Barbara testified at the trials and was a very competent witness.

Four of the Family members who had attempted to put Barbara away were initially charged with attempted murder, but the charge was ultimately reduced to a misdemeanor and the four were sentenced to 90 days in jail. Ouisch failed to appear for trial. She had gone to Carson City and the district attorney's office thought it not worth the trouble to extradite her. Murder was cheap in Los Angeles in those days.

Paul Watkins, the Family member who had left the Family to join

Paul Crockett, the miner, in Shoshone, after the Family had been arrested at the Barker Ranch, went to visit them in jail, after they were transferred to Los Angeles. He tried to help those who had not been arrested but fell out of favor after giving testimony in the Tate-LaBianca murders.

In March, the Inyo authorities heard a rumor that Paul Watkins was going to be killed by the Family. Three days later, he was pulled out of a flaming Volkswagen camper and taken to Los Angeles General Hospital with burns on his face, arms, and back. He told police he had been reading by candlelight and either the candle or a marijuana cigarette he had been smoking caused the blaze. Watkins also admitted that he was only guessing; he was unsure of the origin of the blaze.

In May of 1970, at Shoshone, Crockett, Poston and Watkins encountered Clem, Gypsy, and a youth named Kevin, the newest Family recruit. Clem told Watkins, "Charlie says that when he gets out of jail, you all had better not be around the desert."

On May 31, Death Valley rangers found the body of a hippie in the sand dunes about a mile northeast of the Stovepipe Wells resort. The body was clad in overalls, had long black hair, and was thought to be male. There was no identification. There was forty-five cents in a pocket. Insects had consumed most of the body and the victim has not been positively identified, nor has the cause of death ever been established.

There is no proof that the person was a member of or associated with the Family, but members had been back in the Death Valley area.

Ronald Hughes represented Leslie Van Houton in the Tate-LaBianca trials. He was an unkempt hippie, but he enjoyed a good reputation in the legal community. It was generally known that Manson determined who the defense lawyers would be. He even attempted to dismiss them and act in his own defense. It appeared Hughes had fallen from Charlie's favor because of his effort to win acquittal for Van Houten.

On November 10, 1970, after a weekend recess of the trials, Hughes was missing. He often spent weekends camping at Sespe Hot Springs some 130 miles northwest of Los Angeles. Authorities learned that Hughes had gone to Sespe on Friday with two seventeen-year-olds, James Forsher and Lauren Elder, in Elder's Volkswagen. They were questioned, but not held.

Heavy rains and bad weather prevented a helicopter search for two days after Hughes disappeared. Ground searches proved fruitless and the rumor grew that Hughes had skipped. A more persistent rumor was that he had been murdered by the Family. No evidence of this existed, however.

An odd coincidence, if such it was, occurred on December 2, just four days after Hughes disappeared. Fugitives Bruce Davis and Nancy Pitman, also known as Brenda McCann, surrendered to police. Pitman had been missing for several weeks after failing to appear for sentencing on a forgery charge. Davis had been involved in both the Hinman and Shea murders and was the chief suspect in the slayings of the Scientology students, James Sharp and Doreen Gaul. Prosecutors felt that in some way the disappearance of Hughes and the surrender of Davis and Pitman were related.

In March of 1971, Ventura County sheriff's officers reported finding a body believed to be that of Hughes. It was badly decomposed, wedged face-down between two boulders in Sespe Creek miles from where Hughes had last been seen alive.

On November 8, 1972, a hiker near the Russian River resort of Gunernville in northern California saw a hand protruding from the ground. Exhumation of the body revealed it to be that of a youth in Marine uniform. He had been shot and decapitated. He was subsequently identified as James T. Willett, twenty-six, a former Marine from Los Angeles County. A few days later police spotted Willett's station wagon parked in front of a house in Stockton. After being refused entry the police broke in, arrested two men and two women, and confiscated a number of pistols and shotguns.

The two men were escapees from state prison and the two women were Family members, Priscilla Cooper and Nancy Pitman. While the officers were at the house, a third woman called and asked to be picked up. Police obliged. It was Squeaky Fromme.

Noticing freshly-turned earth in the basement, the police dug and uncovered the body of Lauren Willett, 19, who had been shot in the head. Priscilla Cooper told police that Lauren had killed herself playing Russian roulette, but the skeptical Stockton cops filed murder charges. The men pleaded guilty and were sentenced to seven years. Cooper and Pitman, who Manson once called the Family's chief assassin, got five years. For lack of sufficient evidence, the charges against Squeaky were dropped. The Willetts had been associated with the Family for at least a year, possibly longer, but the motive for their murder was not determined. Perhaps James and Lauren Willett knew too much about another murder.

On November 27, 1970, a James Forsher and a Lauren Elder drove Ronald Hughes to Sespe Hot Springs. After Hughes disappeared, the pair was questioned but not polygraphed. Those investigating the Willett murders were of the opinion that James Forsher and James Willett would have been twenty-four in 1970 and not seventeen. But Lauren was nineteen in 1972, and so would have been seventeen in 1970, a coincidence, perhaps.

Rumors persisted during the Tate-LaBianca trials that the Family was planning to break Manson out, and its members were stockpiling weapons and ammunition toward this effort. After closing time on August 21, 1970, six armed robbers entered the Western Supplies store in the Los Angeles suburb of Hawthorne. While one kept a female clerk and two customers covered with a shotgun, the others began carrying rifles, shotguns and pistols to a van parked in the alley outside. They had collected 140 guns when they spotted the first police car. Alerted by a silent alarm, the Los Angeles Police had already sealed off the alley.

The robbers came out shooting. In the ten-minute gun battle that followed, the van was riddled with more than fifty bullets and some two hundred bullets hit police cars. Surprisingly, no one was killed, although three of the suspects were slightly wounded.

All six robbers were Manson Family members. Those apprehended were Mary Brunner, the first member of the Family; Catherine Share, Gypsy; Dennis Rice, Lawrence Bailey or Little Larry, who was present the night the Tate killers left the Spahn Ranch, and an escaped convict, Kenneth Como. Another Family member, Charles Lovett, got away during the gun battle but was apprehended in a short time. Gypsy and Rice had recently been freed after serving ninety days in jail for their part in attempting to silence Barbara Hoyt.

After their arrest, it was learned the same group had been responsible for robbing a Covina beer distributorship on August 13, which netted them $2,600.

A Family member who was in on the planning of the Hawthorne robbery related the fantastic scheme that, using the Hawthorne robbery weapons, the Family planned to hijack a Boeing 747 and kill one passenger every hour until the imprisoned Family members were released.

The trial judge of the Hawthorne robbery labeled the witnesses called by the defense "the biggest collection of murderers in Los Angeles at one time," and ordered the strongest security measures. The convicted killers included Manson, Beausoleil, Atkins, Krenwinkel, Van Houten, Grogan, and Davis. Their presence was unnerving, especially since by this time a Family member had already proved that the security cells of the Hall of Justice were not escape proof.

Kenneth Como hacksawed his way through the steel bars of his thirteenth floor cell in the pre-dawn hours of October 20. He improvised a bed sheet rope to the eighth floor, kicked in a window of the courtroom where a few months earlier Manson and others of the Family had been prosecuted, and departed the building via the stairways. He was picked up by Sandra Good in the Family van, which she later smashed up. Como escaped but was picked up seven hours later. Also arrested for aiding the escape were Squeaky, Brenda, Kitty Lutesinger, and two other Family members, but they were released for lack of evidence.

During the Hawthorne robbery trial, two jurors reported receiving telephone threats that they would be killed if they voted for conviction. These jurors were replaced by alternates. The calls they had received were linked to an unidentified female Family member.

Gypsy and Rice had received only ninety-day sentences for their part in the attempted murder of Barbara Hoyt, but they and their co-defendants found this court less lenient when it came to shooting at police officers. All were charged with two counts of armed robbery. Rice pleaded guilty and was sent to prison; the others were found guilty on both counts. Como was sentenced to fifteen years to life, Gypsy ten years to life, Lovett to two terms of five years to life, Lawrence Bailey and Mary Brunner twenty years to life. Sandra Good was tried for aiding an escape and was given a six-months jail sentence.

Lynette Fromme remained a conspicuous Family personality in most of the ruthless endeavors that led to the others' convictions, and was frequently a spokesman for them, but she was able to avoid arrest and conviction until her ego led her to the senseless act of trying to assassinate President Gerald Ford in Sacramento. Finally, for that crime, she received a prison sentence that isolated her from Family activities for years to come.

The lawlessness carried out by the Mansons spread anxiety and fear through Southern California. Many people yet today hope that the Family's era was a bad dream that had ended. Los Angeles *Times* reporter, Dave Smith had appropriately written in relation to the Manson saga, "To pull the curtain over the Manson case is to deny ourselves any possible hint of where the beast may come from next, and so remain afraid of things that go bump in the night, the way they were in August, 1969."

◄16►
Concern in Inyo

The arrest of twenty-six members of the Manson Family in Death Valley October 10 and 12 of 1969 had an immediate impact on the surrounding communities. Many had regarded the group merely as a dirty, cruddy, thieving bunch of undesirable hippies. In Independence, where the members were most visible, there was a concern and sympathy for some of the Family members. After they were cleaned up and provided alternative clothing at the jail, some of the women were not readily identified by the officers who had arrested them. There was compassion for a few of them; they were exceptionally youthful, even attractive, and did not seem to be criminal by nature.

District Attorney Frank Fowles, his assistant, Buck Gibbens, and special investigator Jack Gardiner, were faced with the prosecution of fourteen Family members. Because of the unstable nature of the suspects and their questionable backgrounds, the case was, in the true sense, a trying episode. It required long days of intensive work by the prosecution to meet the preliminary hearing date of October 21.

Deputy Sheriff Don Ward was a valuable source of information. His taped interviews with miner Paul Crockett and former Family member Brooks Poston were invaluable. Steuber, assisted by other California Highway Patrol officers, conducted interviews with anyone who could aid in establishing backgrounds of Family members, or who might be potential witnesses.

With the jail bulging at the seams with twenty-four suspects, the Inyo County sheriff had his problems. His deputies were overhearing some odd conversations among Family members, and their everyday antics were a departure from that of normal prisoners. The deputies were not used to the four-letter words in common use, especially by the women.

A few days after she was released in Los Angeles, Squeaky Fromme was back in Independence. She carried messages to and from the Family and attended to Charles Manson. She faired pretty well in Independence. Appealing to the county for assistance, she is reported to have been supplied a motel room and meals at county expense. Charges against Sandra Good were dismissed, and she joined Squeaky in freeloading at the taxpayers' expense.

After charges were filed, seven Family members were released and returned to Los Angeles. Charges against Bruce Davis and Zero were dismissed for insufficient evidence on October 27, and they were released from jail a few days later. On November 5, an officer in Venice answered a suicide call at a house on the beach and found a youth lying on a mattress in a bedroom. The deceased was nicknamed Zero and a bullet wound was found in his right temple. Next to the body was a leather holster and a .22- caliber Iver Johnson revolver. According to a man and three girls present, Zero had killed himself playing Russian roulette. These witnesses said that Zero observed the gun and with it in his right hand spun the cylinder as if in jest, placed the muzzle against his right temple and pulled the trigger.

The officers were unaware that all the witnesses had recently been released in Inyo County following the raids. Present were Bruce Davis, Linda Baldwin, Sue Bartell and Catherine Gillies. When questioned separately, they all told essentially the same story. Police accepted the Russian roulette explanation, and the death was ruled a suicide.

It was interesting to note that Davis admitted picking up the revolver, but when police dusted it and the holster for prints, none were found. The revolver was loaded with one spent shell case. Zero, whose true name was John Phillip Haught, had really bucked the odds.

About a week after the story of Manson's involvement in the Tate-LaBianca murders broke in the press, a Los Angeles Times reporter, Jerry Cohen, was contacted in person by a young man who claimed he had been present when Zero was shot. He asserted that Zero hadn't been playing Russian roulette but was shot by one of the young women present. There had been about eight people in the beach house that night, smoking hashish. At another more-recent Family gathering, the same girl sat staring at him for three hours, fingering her knife. The young man had never met Manson, but had heard from other Family members that there were more murders than the police knew about. He was frightened and borrowed $25 from Cohen to go to northern California. He agreed tentatively to testify at a later date. Cohen never learned his name or ever saw him again.

During the preliminary hearings in Inyo County nearly everyone involved in the arrest or knowledgeable regarding Family activities was called upon to testify. Miner Paul Crockett and former Family members Paul Watkins and Brooks Poston were brought to Independence and interrogated further on Family activities, should their testimony be needed. Interviews with community and desert residents were conducted, but the evidence was limited to a large degree to that provided by the arresting officers.

Highway Patrolman Jim Pursell and Park Ranger Dick Powell were the key witnesses; they had the most information, having observed Family members in possession of stolen vehicles and stolen property. CHP Sergeant Ray Hailey and other CHP officers contributed to the identification of stolen property. Chief Ranger Homer Leach outlined a summary of events and apprehension efforts. Patrol Investigator Dave Steuber worked around the clock to assemble statements and information, and Deputy Sheriffs Don Ward and Dennis Cox contributed dates on Family activities. The prosecution was well-aware of the difficulty in trying individuals who were amoral and exhibited no guilt.

Justice of the Peace Ted Gardiner held preliminary hearings for thirteen Family members on twenty charges. Those against Squeaky Fromme were dismissed for lack of sufficient evidence. Leslie Sankston, Nancy Pitman, Minon Minette and Robert Lane were bound over to Superior Court charged with conspiracy and overt acts. Theft charges on all four were dismissed because it could not be shown that they had been in possession of stolen property.

Charles Manson, Minon Minette, Diane Bluestein, and Rachel Morse were bound over on the arson charge stemming from the burning of the Michigan loader. The testimony from Kitty Lutesinger had placed them at the scene on the date of the incident.

Sandra Good, Mary Schwarm, and Rachel Morse were bound over on stolen property charges because of the stolen Ruger pistol found in their possession in the October 10 Barker Ranch raid. Several charges against others of the Family were dismissed for lack of evidence, and the fact that some were juveniles mandated certification to juvenile court.

Within a short time, the magnitude of the effort to prosecute Manson Family members in the Tate-LaBianca murders diminished the importance of the Inyo County charges. Initial pleas of "not guilty" to the Inyo charges were entered, and those bound over were given continuance. On November 6, LaBianca detectives Patchett and Sartuchi, accompanied by Lt. Burdick of the Los Angeles Police Department, interviewed Family members in Independence, including Manson and Leslie Van Houten, but they were so unimpressed by what they heard that they failed to write up a report on their interview with Manson. It wasn't until November 17 that investigators of the Tate-LaBianca murders established the Manson Family as prime suspects in the homicides. There followed almost immediately investigative visits, followed up by the media. They were preparing for the announcement by Chief of Police Davis of the breaking of the case on December 1.

Subpoenas began to arrive in Inyo County for witnesses. Los Angeles police took Gypsy, Ouisch, Brenda, Snake and Leslie Van Houton as either witnesses or suspects to homicide. Three of the girls gave little information; Gypsy refused to testify. Leslie became an important witness. She knew that Katie, Sadie and Linda had gone to the Tate residence. She was held at the Sybil Brand Institute as a suspect to homicide.

Diane Lake had given her age as twenty, but she was actually only sixteen. Gibbens and Gardiner treated her with kindness and understanding, and she became an important witness. Jack Gardiner and his wife visited Diane, known as Snake in the Family, several times at the Inyo County jail, and she started telling them details of the Manson involvement which she had not given to the Los Angeles grand jury. She suffered from emotional problems and had occasional LSD flashbacks. Through the intervention of Gibbens and Gardiner, she was sent to Patton State Hospital for treatment, where it was determined that her problems were emotional and not mental. Gardiner and his wife were appointed her foster parents. After the trials, she lived with them and their children at Big Pine until she finished high school.

The pre-emption of the Los Angeles charges depleted the Inyo County jail of Family members. Some charges lingered on; others were dismissed. On December 9, Manson was indicted for murder and taken to Los Angeles, but the Inyo County charges against him remained.

Personnel of the Inyo County Sheriff's Office had the duty of supervising the Family members while they were in jail and escorting them to the nearby justice court for preliminary hearings. The officers were normally tolerant of the strange behavior of the Family. For the most part, Family members were not abused in the jail, but there may have been one partially justified exception. Deputy Don Ward was aware that Charlie had attempted to induce Brooks Poston to go from Barker Ranch to Shoshone to kill Ward and later tried to get Juan Flynn to do the job. Ward had embarrassed Charlie by searching him in front of the girls in Shoshone in early 1969. Ward was assisting at the jail during the first days the Family members were being held. It was standard procedure to handcuff prisoners when escorting them across the street to the court building during preliminary hearings. After one hearing, Ward was taking the handcuffs off Manson in returning him to jail, when Manson made some crack about Ward still being on his death list. Ward, shorter than Charlie but stocky, lost his temper and knocked Manson down. He regained his composure and apologized.

Threats from Family members were not unusual. Fromme, Good and other girls staying in town were talking about the people who they were marking for disposition. At first the threats were treated lightly, but when the Family became connected with the Hinman, Shea, Tate and LaBianca murders, those who had any part in the Manson experience in Inyo County began to take the threats seriously.

Paul Crockett was obviously on Charlie's death list, and he felt Poston and Watkins were also in danger. After the preliminary hearings, Ward immediately took the three back to Shoshone where they were reasonably safe. The townspeople were not happy to have ex-Manson Family members living in their community and even attempted to submit a petition to have them removed. Ward succeeded in placating the community and became the protector of the trio.

He was influential in helping them move into town, and they became gainfully employed with the Charles Brown Company, which operated most of the services in the community. They dug ditches, painted buildings, repaired sewers and poured concrete, but resentment did not totally subside. Throughout the ordeal, Ward seemed to understand their plight; he continued to defend them and became a close friend.

Encouraged by Crockett, Poston started a combo band and played frequently in Inyo County, including Tecopa and Lone Pine. Watkins was also a musician and played with the group occasionally. Poston later expanded his musical effort and played engagements in the Lake Tahoe, Carson City and Reno areas.

To everyone's loss, Don Ward became ill with cancer and died Thanksgiving Day, 1976. Many came to pay their respects to this stout-hearted lawman, but the most visible and audible at the final ceremony was Brooks Poston, Jane Boltinghouse and David Wells, who provided touching musical acknowledgement to a departed friend. Their musical composition, "Stormy Clouds," was especially narrated and sung in tribute to Ward.

Many people were deeply involved in Inyo County with the Manson Family apprehension. Most displayed little concern with what they believed to be idle threats, but when the situation was tense, fatiguing or threatening, most displayed a wonderful sense of humor that helped to lighten their situation. The California Highway Patrol members, who were accustomed to such conditions, were especially good at easing tensions. Officers Hailey and Manning were never at a loss to supply humorous incidents when the conversation warranted. On October 10, 1969, when some of the female Family members wondered how they were to be transported out of such a difficult area, Manning told them not to worry because there was a DC-3 parked just over the hill to fly them out. The truth was you couldn't have landed a Piper Cub anywhere near the area. When Doug Manning suggested dropping Charlie down a one hundred-foot mine shaft, Family members were amused, but not Charlie.

Officers at Barker ranch brought out the broom that Deputy Don

Ward had accidently blasted with his shotgun. They sawed off the handle, framed the broom, and gave it to Don as the only casualty at Barker Ranch.

Mel Reese operated the Western Auto Supply store in Lone Pine and also provided telegraph wire service. The Manson girls frequently used the wire service to send for money, and waited around for replies.

Reese said, "They came in wearing the darndest outfits; sometimes long sack dresses dragging the ground or skirts so short they barely covered their butts. They hardly ever wore any undergarments, bras, or panties. One day four of the girls came down to send telegrams and were waiting around for replies. All were wearing extremely short dresses and were sitting on a bench with everything exposed. An elderly town matron came in and, in shock and exasperation, demanded of me, 'What kind of a store are you running here?' and just as if I had hollered attention," Mel said, "all the girls stood up."

On December 1, when Chief of Police Davis announced in Los Angeles that the Tate-LaBianca suspects had been determined and subsequent complaints had been issued for their arrest, the media remained suspicious about the Death Valley investigations and began to show a big interest in what had transpired there. CHP Officer Jim Pursell was interviewed at Furnace Creek and was later flown by helicopter to Barker Ranch for photographs. After that a fairly accurate release was made to the public. Pursell's influence soothed some ruffled feathers because previous stories about Death Valley had been inaccurate.

The $25,000 reward offered for information leading to the arrest of suspects in the Tate homicides appeared up for grabs. The press speculated about who in Death Valley had been the first to realize the Manson Family were suspect. Pursell inferred that Dick Powell had relayed his first suspicion to Pursell on September 29; this was the date on which Crockett and Poston at Barker Ranch had given some intriguing revelations about the Family's involvement in drugs, sex and satanic worship. Powell had been following press coverage of the Tate-LaBianca murders in detail and offered his speculations on the matter to Pursell that night.

Powell, dedicated and conscientious, had combed the desert day and night, looking for those responsible for the burning of the Michigan loader. Young, eager, and aggressive, Powell was regarded by his peers as a combination mountain goat and greyhound. When the San Bernardino Sun headlined that Powell, a park ranger, was eligible for the $25,000 reward, he said he could not accept the reward because he was officially on duty and being paid by the government for his work. Jim Pursell offered the same reason when it was suggested that he, as the man who had lifted Manson out from under the bathroom cabinet, should receive the reward. Pursell was on duty as a highway patrolman during the pursuit of the Family. Actually both Powell and Pursell had performed hours of uncompensated overtime, and it is likely that they could have logically accepted and shared the reward.

Roman Polanski's attorney, working with Los Angeles police, divided the reward: $12,000 each to Ronnie Howard and Virginia Graham, cellmates of Susan Atkins, and $1,000 to Steven Weiss, who found the .22-caliber murder weapon.

After members of the Family had been subpoenaed to Los Angeles on the felony warrants, there remained the possibility that a few members might still be hidden out in the desert, living from caches similar to those found at Barker Ranch and Anvil Springs. Such violent characters as Bruce Davis and Clem (Steve Grogan) were out on bail. They had been identified and were wanted by Los Angeles authorities, but it was rumored that they were back in Death Valley.

There also remained the possibility that stolen property, unaccounted for, had remained in the desert. Unmarked graves of victims of the deadly Family were still rumored. Fowles and his assistant, Gibbens, ordered repeated searches of the desert and with the support of the Los Angeles area law enforcement team, went up every major canyon on the west side of the Panamint Mountains.

Game Warden Vern Burandt guided FBI Agent Bill Swanson of Sacramento into the canyons around Panamint City, the ghost town above Ballarat, looking for one of the ten most wanted criminals who was reported by a reliable witness to be living up there. It was not definitely established that he was one of the Manson tribe, but it was suspected.

It was reported that Catherine Share, Gypsy, and other members of the Family were in Goler Wash and Warm Springs Canyon with a Los Angeles film crew. Commercial photography companies operate under permits from the National Park Service, and no such permit had been issued. Pursell and Gibbens were in the area when they were joined by Chief Ranger Leach in Warm Spring Canyon and Butte Valley. They encountered Gypsy and the film crew. She immediately launched into a tirade against the intrusion.

"You are the hunters and we are the hunted, but you've got a mark on your head and some day we'll be the hunters and you'll be the hunted," she threatened.

The deaths of Zero in Venice, California, and Joel Pugh in London, attributed to the Manson Family, were quickly communicated to the Inyo officials, and their fears were aggravated by the verbal innuendos of Squeaky Fromme and Sandra Good. Because of the hideous

Furnace Creek Ranch, date palms and golf course. Robert Murphy photo.

nature of the Hinman, Shea, Tate and LaBianca crimes, precautions were taken by a number of individuals. District Attorney Fowles and his assistant, Buck Gibbens, moved their families to the Bay area for a time, and for a while, they lived together at the Gibbens residence.

Family members who had been released from jail or who were out on bail in Los Angeles occasionally drifted back to Owens Valley and Death Valley. Scroungy characters of the same kind showed up in various places all over the Valley, including Shoshone. Three men in a brown van came looking for Crockett and Poston and the same van was seen in the Furnace Creek area. Others were observed at Wildrose Ranger Station where Dick and Sheila Powell lived; they were so edgy that Sheila started traveling with her husband so she would not be alone at the ranger station. Strangers were seen in the park Service residential area at Furnace Creek where Jim Pursell and his wife lived, and it became known that many rangers and others slept with loaded rifles and shotguns beside their beds.

One day government wives observed an old van with several long-haired passengers cruising slowly through their area. Word of this spread. About midnight that night, a strong wind storm started blowing in from the south. Clouds of swirling sand filled the air, and the tamarisk trees in the housing area began swaying with a swish, swish sound. About 2:30 a.m., in one section of the area, there came a loud plop, plop, plop, and then silence; fifteen seconds later plop, plop; thirty seconds later, plop, plop, plop, and then silence again for two or three minutes. It sounded like someone was hitting the side of a house with a flat board, but it seemed to be moving.

The night was very dark. Visibility was obscured by blowing sand. Again, the plop, plop sound echoed in the street. Finally in the direct illumination of a street light, residents nearby saw a huge cardboard box being blown over and over down the asphalt street. Not a light came on, but there were at least two male residents standing in the shadows of their residences; one had a fully loaded shotgun.

For more than a year after the arrests of the Manson Family, rangers, CHP officers, and deputy sheriffs kept a vigilant watch on Death Valley; despite rhetoric of editorial writers that the Empire State Building could have been hidden in that section of the desert, and it would not have been noticed.

In the end, their unconventional habits, twisted psyches, and drugs spelled the Family's doom. Deputy Don Ward searched Charlie on one of the first times he came to Shoshone, and Deputy Dennis Cox picked up Diane Lake only four days after the Family members had arrived at Hannum Ranch from Los Angeles.

Had Charlie and his Family stayed in the populous urban areas, they may have lived more securely. They were not part of the desert and were naked in its environment. The harsh desert did not treat them kindly. Their cohesiveness was destroyed. Members defected with fears which they could neither understand nor endure.

The fear the Family engendered in Inyo County has subsided, and tranquility has returned to the Valley. Yet the question remains: Who knows how many more killings might have followed if a comparatively few park rangers, highway patrolmen, and sheriff's deputies in the sparsely populated Inyo County desert had not persisted in finding out who and why anyone would torch an almost new front-end loader?

Street-wise Charlie Manson and the lost "children" of his Family had no rapport with the harsh reality of the desert. Where his dune buggies once roared in puny imitation of Rommel's elite corps, today's occasional visitor may shut off the engine of his four-wheel drive, and hear nothing, not even the sound of the wind.

◄17►
An Update

In many respects, the Manson saga reflects certain parallels with the attitudes and functions of religious cults. There is most always some reference to the Biblical millennium or Armageddon, or at least some eminent near-term disaster. There is the dominance of a cultist leader over unfortunate and gullible individuals, and a departure from currently accepted social and moral values.

At this writing there are a number of fanatical religious cults which can be likened in this manner to the Manson family. They employ programming, fear, guilt, eminent doom, and a strong leader whereby unfortunates are lured into such a fold with a guarantee of passage to heaven. The Satanist employs the sordid secret world of devil worship, including animal and human sacrifices. The Church of Scientology is a cult that extracts sizeable amounts of money from its members and intimidates its enemies. Its reportedly 8 million members must be "cleared" by being successfully put through training sessions based on the philosophy of founder L. Ron Hubbard. They also retain a stockpile of weapons and surveillance equipment. The Hare Krishnas have employed the use of drugs, kidnapping, and beatings to protect an illegal multimillion dollar enterprise. The Church Universal & Triumphant in Montana is a sect with vast ranch properties that includes an array of protective measures including numerous bomb shelters. The central main shelter is designed to house over 700 members with food and fuel supplies to reportedly last several years. In 1989, the husband of Elizabeth Clare Prophet, their leader, and a security guard were arrested by federal authorities and convicted of illegally purchasing weapons and ammunition. Prophet, also known as Guru Ma, claims over 100,000 members around the world.

Although some authorities have stated that Manson's formulated policy had little relationship to existing religious cults, it must be remembered that Manson was an eclectic, a borrower of ideas. The "mystique" that draws followers into these organizations or groups is not readily identifiable. The social and moral deterioration of family values is no doubt a contributing factor. Often the unfortunates, frequently the younger set, who find it difficult to accept the establishment, the political system, and who fail to conform with social norms, fall from grace and are vulnerable to such invitation.

Charles Milles Manson, after 25 years in prison, continues to cast images of murder and mayhem associated with the Family. The fascination with his mystique is unblurred. His legendary eyes have not aged despite the years. In a now sallow aged face, they remain bright, black and haunting.

On April 19, 1971, Manson was originally sent to Death Row in San Quentin. After the death penalty was initially abolished by the Supreme Court, Manson was transferred to Folsom Prison in September 1972. In early 1974, prison officials reported Manson was possibly entering a regressive state, and he was transported to a psychiatric prison facility at Vacaville, Calif. for evaluation. Although he remained at Folsom following treatment, he was eventually placed in 1976 at the Vacaville prison for a nine-year stay. Manson was then transferred to the state prison at San Quentin on July 19, 1985. He was lately moved to the new federal prison at Corcoran, California.

Others of the Manson Family remain in varying confining institutions. Both Charles "Tex" Watson (Tate-LaBianca murders) and Bruce Davis (Hinman-Shorty Shea murders) are confined at the California Men's Colony in San Luis Obispo, Calif. Watson has become the senior inmate serving in the Protestant Chapel as acting minister, counseling inmates and receiving special privileges. Since his confinement he has married, fathered 3 children, and lives in a trailer within the prison. Davis acts as assistant minister and counselor in the medium security prison.

Inmates complained during recent interviews that Watson has ordered administrative discipline against fellow inmates who have objected to his teaching and his running of the church. It is reported that the Reverend Stanley McGuire, civilian chaplain assigned to the prison since 1967, was hardly ever there. He had been accused by inmates of not only allowing Watson and his associates to take over the Plazaview Chapel, but also of ignoring complaints about their behavior. Prison program director and public information officer Larry Kamien supported McGuire's actions, but the latter did eventually resign his post at the prison with full retirement benefits.

Deputy District Attorney Steven Kay, who prosecuted Davis for the 1969 killings and has attended parole hearings of these people for 20 years stated, "It is wrong for these two people to be running the Protestant Chapel." Watson also heads "Abounding Love Ministries" through which he receives donations from inside and outside the prison. Kay has noted the acronym for the ministry is ALMS, and has observed that no doubt Watson "makes a lot of money at that." Prison officials, however, dismiss complaints from inmates as stemming from jealousy and personality clashes among rivals in the prison. Although his official job designation is senior clerk, chapel literature lists Watson as minister and Davis as associate pastor.

In 1975, Sandra Good and Squeaky Fromme lived in a rundown apartment on P Street in Sacramento. As they continued to be the antenna for Manson, it was necessary that they be near him (he was at that time housed in Folsom Prison). Manson at this time was communicating ecological and environmental concerns to whomever would listen, especially Sandra and Squeaky. This change in philosophy was not really a drift towards non-violence; Manson was miffed at President Nixon's comment of guilt during the Los Angeles trials. Squeaky and Sandra appeared in their hooded red robes at the Sacramento news offices to deliver a press release entitled "Manson is Mad at Nixon".

The text was compiled from Manson's writings. Contained therein was the threat, "if Nixon is really wearing a new face [i.e. President Ford] and continues to run this country against the law, your homes will be bloodier than the Tate-LaBianca houses." It exhorted other violence may occur, but was received with such inattentiveness by the media that Squeaky was no doubt spurred to grim escalation.

Ford's visit to the state capitol in Sept. 1975, was no secret. The night of Sept. 4, Ford slept on the sixth floor of the Senator Hotel, just a half-mile from the frustrated Sandra and Squeaky. Ford spoke to a packed breakfast gathering and left at 9:55 a.m. for a stroll to the capitol grounds and a meeting with Gov. Brown. Squeaky donned a bright red floor length gown, placed a .45 caliber hand gun well hidden in her cover, and walked a little over eight blocks to the capitol grounds. The President appeared, and people lined up and began to applaud. Squeaky pushed through the crowd until she was just a few feet away from the President. Larry Buendorf, former Naval Intelligence Officer and now secret service agent, instantly batted the gun away, grabbed the weapon and shoved Squeaky to the ground. Sgt. Gleason of the Los Angeles Sheriff's Office would later comment, "Squeaky had no intention of hurting Ford. She knew how to operate that gun. We have pictures of her and Mary Brunner firing weapons that we'd picked up over the years. So they were both familiar with the weapons. Squeaky just wanted to get Manson's name in the paper..." Squeaky did pick up a lot of publicity. She was on the cover of the Sept. 15, 1975 issue of *Time,* and in *Newsweek* the same week. On Dec. 19, 1975, she was sentenced to life imprisonment. She was transferred from the federal penitentiary in Pleasanton, Calif., to the maximum security prison at Alderson, West Virginia in Aug. 1979.

On September 11, 1975, Sandra Good released a list of several governmental and business leaders and companies, saying they were marked for death if they didn't stop polluting the earth. She consequently stood trial in March 1976 for conspiracy to mail "ecology kill letters" and received a 10-year sentence. Paroled in 1985, she was last reported living at Bridport, Vermont, having her identity discovered when she became involved in a protest against the International Paper Company's pollution of air and water.

In November, 1977, Sergeant Gleason (L.A. Sheriff's Office) was contacted by a lieutenant at the prison in Tracy, Calif., where Steve "Clem" Grogan was housed. He was informed that Grogan wanted to talk and reveal the location of Shorty Shea's body, as he was being denied parole, and was bidding for a deal. Gleason and his partner went to talk to Grogan and eventually flew him down to Los Angeles. Clem was taken to the burned out Spahn Ranch and he showed them where the body was buried, at the base of a steep embankment.

Officers were impressed with Grogan's change, because of all the male members of the Manson family, he was originally the most disoriented, a zombie and really bonkers. He went to school in prison, showed an interest in airplanes, and became a licensed airframe and engine mechanic.

The officers waited a month before digging for Shorty because they didn't want to put pressure on Grogan in prison for snitching. They eventually did go out one afternoon and started digging with shovels, and after a couple hours they found Shea's remains. The skeleton was intact, thus severing a key Family legend—Shea had not been decapitated and cut up into nine pieces. Gleason surmised it "was just a story, dreamed up to frighten the girls and keep everybody from talking." The recovery of Shea's body was in one sense a relief, as there had always been the faint dread that Shorty Shea might one day show up alive and really embarrass the prosecution.

Ruth Ann Morehouse, the famous Quisch, was arrested in October, 1975, on a four year warrant for the Honolulu dopeburger caper during the Manson trial. She was to have been sentenced back in April of 1971, but she was nearly nine months pregnant, and she fled to Carson City. Later she married and had another child. At the time of her 1975 arrest she was still wearing the bandages from plastic surgery which removed the hideous X on her forehead. She wanted no part of the Family and had become a stern mother.

In July, 1976, Leslie Van Houten received an evaluation by a consultant for the California Institute of Women which in summary stated, "there are no contradictions for parole consideration." Subsequently, a California Court of Appeals dismissed her conviction.

The 84 pages of appeal opinion were written by Judge J. Vogel for the three-judge panel. Although only one part of the appeal was accepted, it was sufficient to order a new trial for Leslie Van Houten.

Van Houten's retrial began in March, 1977, and lasted four months. Deputy District Attorney Steven Kay was the prosecutor. The jury was deadlocked in July, and another new trial was ordered. Van Houten continued to be held in Sybil Brand jail until December 27, when she was released on $200,000 bail which was raised by friends and relatives. She had a temporary freedom and worked as a secretary for a lawyer, and lived with a female author.

Her third trial began in March, 1978. She hoped for a manslaughter or second degree murder conviction, which would have allowed her to be set free on time served. Van Houten admitted killing Mrs. LaBianca, but defense psychiatrists had concluded that she should be found guilty of manslaughter due to diminished mental capacity caused by mental illness.

The prosecution introduced twenty photographs of Leno and Rosemary LaBianca. The ghastly pictures and bloody testimony of coroner Dr. Thomas Noguchi were most disturbing to the jurors. The photo of Mr. LaBianca's throat with a knife embedded in it is probably one of the most horrifying shots in the history of photography. The day after the Fourth of July Van Houten was convicted—not of manslaughter, but first degree murder.

A few days later Patricia Krenwinkel came up for parole. On his own, without instructions from the district attorney, Stephen Kay made an appearance at the July 17 hearing. Kay had recently refreshed himself on the facts of the case in Van Houten's trial and could, therefore, deliver a bloody, knife slashing recitation of the murders, which horrified the Community Release Board. It took Kay about two hours to recount Krenwinkel's part in the murder.

Mr. Kay began appearing at virtually all the Manson Family parole hearings. His résumé indicates that he was the first district attorney in California to attend a parole hearing to oppose release of a defendant serving a life sentence. Over the next ten years he would attend 35 Manson group hearings.

For her release hearing in 1982, Leslie Van Houten had acquired 900 signatures on a petition seeking her freedom. Alarmed by this, Mr. Kay contacted Sharon Tate's mother, Doris. Mrs. Tate recalls Kay saying, "You always said you would help, and I need your help now." Until then she had gone through a long and painful mourning.

After Mr. Kay's phone call, Mrs. Tate became a powerful citizen activist on behalf of the victims and their relatives of violent crime. She began work on a cumulative list, of those opposed to the release of any of the murderers of Circle Drive or Waverly Place. The list ultimately stood at over 300,000 and was sent by the box load to the parole board. She also campaigned for Proposition 8, the "Victim's Bill of Rights", which was approved by California voters in 1982.

The year 1984 marked the first time survivors and relatives could make impact statements at parole hearings in California under the strictures of Proposition 8. Doris Tate brought 350,000 signatures with her when she came to Tex Watson's hearing to oppose his release. Although Doris Tate has recently died, a daughter is carrying on this very dedicated effort.

On Sept. 25, 1984, Manson was in the hobby shop at the Vacaville psychiatric prison when one Jan Holmstrom doused him with paint thinner and set him on fire. Manson was reportedly objecting to Holmstrom's chanting of the Hare Krishna mantra. Manson suffered burns over 18% of his body, the worst affecting his face, hands and scalp.

On December 23, 1987, Squeaky Fromme was reported missing at a bed check in the penitentiary at Alderson, West Virginia. She had learned that Manson might have cancer and reportedly wanted to be near him. The front page headlines of *The Post* in New York City read, "Prez Ford Assailant Flees Jail." Fromme had been corresponding with Manson for over five years. She had refused parole stating with satisfaction, "My love's in jail, I'm in jail." On Christmas Day she was discovered in a wooded area about two miles from the prison. After her arrest authorities transferred Fromme to a more secure federal facility at Lexington, Kentucky, and an additional fifteen months were added to her sentence for the December breakout.

Linda Kasabian, the girl Manson sent to kill at the Tate home, but who refused in horror, is raising her four children in New England.

On Nov. 8, 1988, 40-year-old Patricia Krenwinkel was denied parole a seventh time. "The degree of barbaric, violent behavior has no equal," Commissioner Rudolph Caspro said after the two-hour hearing.

What about the great team of Los Angeles Sheriff's Detectives Whiteley and Guenther who helped so much in Inyo County and Death Valley to bring the Manson group to justice? Sometime in the 1970s Sergeant Whiteley transferred out of homicide into vice detail. In the summer of 1988 he injured his back during a raid, and after 32 years, retired. Deputy Guenther has also retired, and wants to keep his memories stored. A fellow officer commented, "He really wants to forget this case. I don't really blame him—what a creepy case."

Many of the Inyo County and Death Valley officials involved in the local Manson episode remain of interest. Frank Fowles, former D.A., is now in private practice in Bishop, Calif. Buck Gibbons, former assistant district attorney, is now D.A. at Independence, Calif. County officials as well as private citizens have many curios of that era. There is talk of some day gathering the Manson Family memorabilia and depositing it in the local museum. Like other officials who investigated the Family, Fowles was proud of former member Paul Watkins who became politically active and appeared on TV in anti-drug and anti-cult programs. Paul Watkins unfortunately died of cancer a few years ago at the age of 43. Additionally, Brooks Poston has finally been able to go on with his life, and plays in a band around Carson City and Reno, Nevada.

District attorney investigator Jack Gardiner has died. He and his wife were foster parents of Diane Lake, putting her through Big Pine High School and afterward in secretarial training. She is no doubt the star of rehabilitation, entering bank employment at various locations in Northern California. She has married and is basically now a corporate executive.

Merrill Curtis, the Inyo County Sheriff, died this past year and is buried in Bishop, Calif. Most of the deputy sheriffs of 1969 have moved on to other locations. Dennis Cox, deputy at Lone Pine, was last reported to be in Barrow, Alaska with the U.S. Public Health Service.

Dave Steuber, Chief Auto Theft Investigator for the CHP out of Fresno, Calif., was a witness to both raids at the Barker Ranch in 1969. His taped interviews of Kitty Lutesinger and others provided the key relationship between the Barker Ranch arrests and the homicide events in the Los Angeles area. His real contributions were not especially noted by the media but his testimony at the Los Angeles trials was most essential. He is retired and doing part time investigative work for a district attorney's office in Northern California.

Game Warden Vern Burandt retired from the Fish & Game Dept. and was, by last report, living in Inyo County.

California Highway Patrol officers have gone in many different directions. Lt. H.M. (Chico) Hurlburt retired as commander of the Bishop area and now lives in Nevada. Officer Alan B. George left the CHP and joined the Inyo County Sheriff's Department, and lately was elected Sheriff of that county. Officer Dennis Journigan also left the CHP and was last reported to be employed by the Nevada Livestock Inspection Board. Officer Jack O'Neil retired and is now employed in part time maintenance with the Inyo National Forest. Officer Monty Parker retired and lives in Montana, where he operates his own trucking business. Officer Doug Manning is still active on the force as Senior Traffic Officer in the Bishop area command, and lives in Lone Pine, Calif. Officer Ben Anderson retired and currently lives in Colorado.

CHP Officer Ray Hailey, in charge of the Lone Pine post in 1969, provided leadership in the Manson Family arrests in Death Valley and was one of the key people in promoting this story. He is retired and lives in Bakersfield, California. CHP Officer Jim Pursell, who contributed so much to this story, was promoted to sergeant and spent two years in Van Nuys, Calif. He returned to Inyo County and served in the Bishop Command Post until retirement.

Of the National Park Service personnel involved in the 1969 Manson episode, there has been a complete change. Chief Park Ranger Homer Leach transferred to Redwoods National Park and is now retired in Northern California. Al Schneider, district ranger, transferred to Lassen Volcanic National Park as Chief Ranger. He is now retired and lives in Red Bluff, Calif. Don Carney, north district ranger, transferred to Voyagers National Park, is now retired and living in Wisconsin. Dick Powell, ranger at Wildrose, transferred to Sequoia National Park and later to the Rocky Mountain Regional Office in Denver as Safety Officer. Rangers Paul Fodor and Earl Curran have transferred out of Death Valley, but are still active as park rangers.

Charles Tobin, maintenance supervisor who flew several days during the Manson search, transferred to Yellowstone National Park. He is retired and lives in Livingston, Montana. Kerby Sims, maintenance foreman, and present at the burning of the Michigan loader in Death Valley in September, 1969, has retired and lives in Arizona. He remains active in lapidary work.

The author, who served as superintendent of Death Valley National Monument during Manson's activity and capture there, later transferred to Lassen Volcanic National Park. He is now retired and lives near Livingston, Montana.

What began in Death Valley as a simple charge of arson soon escalated to illegal firearms, stolen credit cards, and auto thefts. Originally, the young people were regarded as "unfortunates", exhibiting no dangerous confrontations with the officers involved in the arrest of the 26 Family members. As the tragic events began to unfold and Los Angeles officials came to Inyo County seeking suspects, the local concern mounted. In fear and horror, the inhabitants of Death Valley and Inyo County heard and watched as events they could hardly believe came to light in the grisly Los Angeles trials. Though time has a way of diminishing the concern, fear, and frustration in dealing with episodes involving homicides of such a gruesome nature, images occasionally return, and we relive a bit of the story. With them comes the ever recurring question—why did this happen?

Biography

Robert J. Murphy is a thirty-two-year veteran of the National Park Service. When he retired from the Park Service several years ago, he was awarded the much-prized Meritorious Service Award of the Department of the Interior. His expertise earned commendations in wildlife management, forest fire control, and public relations.

Murphy's perseverance and cooperative leadership in tracing the activities of the Manson Family led to their apprehension and arrest in Death Valley and, finally, to their conviction for theft and murder in Los Angeles.

Bob Murphy has written informative tracts and articles about some of the outstanding features of the National Parks in which he has served. He is an honorary director of the 49er's Club in Death Valley, and has actively pursued land acquisition that has enhanced the value of Death Valley National Monument. Howard J. Chapman, Western Regional Director of the National Park Service, said of Bob Murphy, "It's people like Bob Murphy who made the National Park Service the outstanding organization it is today. His knowledge, his experience and his tremendous dedication will be sorely missed."

Bob Murphy was born and raised in Montana attending high school and college in Bozeman. He and his wife Alice lived in eight states in serving the National Park Service.